OPEN ME

*The true story of a magical journey
from fear to freedom*

To Denise

Shining star sister —
What a delight to
connect with you ⌣

May you always
remember the angels are
always singing for you.
awaiting your command.
love ya! xx
Denise

OPEN ME

*The true story of a magical journey
from fear to freedom*

LEANNE BABCOCK

FIVE FEATHER PUBLISHING

Book production:
DIYPublishing.co.nz

©Leanne Babcock 2017
Five Feather Publishing
ISBN 978-0-473-39067-9

For anyone who has ever had self-doubt

Reviews for Open Me

"Leanne's book made me feel like I was participating in the intimate journey of her evolving soul as she openly shares her heart. She's a natural story teller and any reader will enjoy this river of life that she recounts."

Blair Styra, spiritual channel for Tabaash.

"*Open Me* has all the ingredients of a wonderfully inspirational book—a true story, told with honesty, openness, and vulnerability. Already I have been inspired to make changes in my life."

Kim Chamberlain, author & speaker

"*Open Me* is a radiant reflection of personal turmoil, sadness, and fear unearthed and transformed into courage, joy and profound love.

Linda Christina Beauregard, speaker, author—*I Gave Myself Cancer, I Can Take It Away! Alternatives Brought Me Back to Life*

"We all have times in our lives when we feel off-kilter or off-track. We all suffer from self-doubt. Leanne has looked inside herself and examined her true purpose —such a journey takes courage and commitment and is not for the fainthearted. This book will help anyone who wants to do the same."

Melissa Clark-Reynolds, Officer of the New Zealand Order of Merit

"Leanne has written an honest and compelling story of her fears, challenges and truths, taking me with her and allowing me to remember my own. She encourages all women to wake up to what they may be avoiding and to trust their own spirit."

Kaya Singer, artist, mentor, author—*Wiser & Wilder*

Contents

Acknowledgements

My heart overflows with gratitude towards so many people, who have helped me each in their own way, as I took these steps along this path of writing my first book. I will always hold you in my heart.

Thank you….

Andrew Rundle-Keswick, Anna Groves, Annette Esquenet, Anthony Baynes, Barb Burnett, Barbara Farfan, Bob O'Connor, Brendan Clegg, Cary Hayward, Catherine Cooper, Carole Harbard, Christine Jurgensen, David Bernard, Debbie Ford, Deidre Hooper, Dorie Hanson, Eileen Oliver-Free, Elizabeth Gilbert, Felicity Yellin, Gordon Babcock, Greg Babcock, Heather Simpson, Helen Emmerson, Irena Stenner, Jon Shutt, Jules Barber, Kris Lockett, Leahna Hardie, Linda Beauregard, Lis Sowerbutts, Lisa Nimmo, Lorraine Marshall-Rey, Louise Barry, Louise Hammond, Maggie Wear, Maia Freeman, Margot Broadhead, Marie LeFebvre, Mary Alice Arthur, Matt Gauldie, Melissa Clark-Reynolds, Pamela Meeking-Stewart, Peter Waugh, Rachel Tobin, Sandra Cosentino, Sarah Dill, Sarah Hayward, Sarah Main, Shane Mercer, Sharon Muir, Sue Kerr, Sue Matthew, Tabaash, Tanette Hickey, Toni Craig, Valamaya Harfield, Verity Jones.

A whole-hearted thank you to my dear dear friend and companion, Anthony, for putting up with me writing in the corner rather than coming out to play, for diligently finding places for me to write in the shade while on road trips, and for submitting yourself to listen for hours of me reading various iterations of my book. And thank you for loving me through this journey.

A special thank you to Katie (Catherine Cooper) who jumped in as my writing coach and editor. Without your help, I could not have done this.

And finally, thank you to Barbara Farfan who sparked me to start this whole ball rolling in the first place.

Chapter Before
The Others

Open Me is the true story of how I opened myself to the whispers of my heart—of how I learned to listen, to trust, to be truly free. It is the story of a journey on which I faced my worst fears, listened to my intuition and the wisdom of nature, and was guided by the trees, stones and birds. Travelling to sacred places around the world, I deepened my exploration of who I am. Magic and miracles began to happen as I found the courage to heal. Finally, I met the challenge of love with newfound freedom, and fearlessly continued to follow the voice of my spirit.

The events described in this book are based on fact, but to respect the privacy of some individuals, most names and identifying details have been changed. For the same reason, and for the sake of simplicity, I have also created several composite characters, combining two or more people into single characters.

I invite you to travel with me on the journey that changed my life. I hope that your heart opens too.

PART 1

Open Me to listen

"I want to live like this."

Chapter 1

I held my green eye pencil steady as I lined my eyelids. I used my baby finger to smudge the lines in just the right places. Peering closer into the mirror, I noticed some new wrinkles. I pulled the skin back to smooth out the creases, then let go.

My attention shifted to my hair. I reached up and wrapped an unruly lock around my finger to make it curl in the direction I wanted. My hair rarely did what I wanted it to do, and if it did, it didn't last for long.

I released the curl from my finger, and ran my hands down the front of my favourite purple gypsy dress, stopping at the small roll of my protruding tummy. I sighed and prodded it. There was nothing to be done about it, at least not in the next ten minutes.

Closing my eyes I placed both my hands over my belly and breathed in deeply to calm my nerves and relax the anxious cramping that often appeared before social gatherings. The discomfort usually disappeared once I started talking with people.

After a few breaths, I opened my eyes and stepped back. I looked good. And when I looked good, I felt good. Confident. In control. I glanced down at my bare feet and the thin, silver ankle bracelet on my left foot. *Nice touch*.

I looked up again, and my eyes met my eyes. I paused

to look a bit deeper. Beyond the makeup, beyond the smile—a glimmer of angst.

I looked away and headed outside.

Stepping onto the deck, I took in a deep breath. *I'm celebrating today.*

It was my big day. My fiftieth birthday. Well, it wasn't really the actual day. My real birthday was six months earlier. I was born under the hot summer sun in Canada, and there was no way I was going to celebrate my fiftieth birthday in the cold New Zealand winter, so I'd decided to wait and have my birthday party in February.

Even though I'd had a few extra months to get used to the idea of this milestone birthday, I was still having a hard time believing it. *How can I be fifty?* In my mind my Mom was fifty and I was still thirty-six. I knew the maths didn't add up but then a lot of things didn't add up in our minds.

I contemplated the female archetypes: the Maiden, the Mother, and the Crone. I was no longer the Maiden and I had skipped being the Mother, having had no children of my own. *Am I a Crone?* I grimaced. Just saying the word conjured up images of an ugly, old woman with a huge crooked nose and warts all over her face.

"Hey birthday girl! Are you coming?" Emily shouted. I smiled. Just the sound of her voice warmed my heart. We'd met thirteen years earlier on a cooking course, and had become dear friends ever since.

Some people had already arrived, and Emily was happily organising them to play relay games on the grass. She was always so good at gathering people together and getting them involved. *Much better than me.*

I watched as she jumped up and down laughing while giving instructions for the next game. *I love how people just love to have fun. It doesn't matter how old we are.*

I laughed and waved. "Be right there!"

My eyes took in the expansive lawn and, beyond it, the almond trees and the stream running through our farm. The day was perfect. The late afternoon sun was still high, and the sky was the brightest blue. Everything was lush and full of life.

After eighteen months living on the almond farm, I was finally starting to like it. If I told anyone else how long it had taken me to enjoy being there, they would have been puzzled. How could anyone not like it? The trees, the flowers, the land. Some would say it was paradise.

When Martin and I sold our house in the city and bought the country property looking for a more "back to the earth" lifestyle, we knew it was going to be hard work, but we were so excited.

When we first moved in, a particular bird call caught my attention. It sounded like the bird was saying, "Very good! Very good! Very good!" I had lived in New Zealand for nearly twenty-two years, and I had heard this bird before, but I hadn't heard it sing those words.

I nicknamed it the Very Good bird.

Maybe I heard that bird singing "Very good" because it was the message I needed to hear over and over again. There were a lot of things at the time that did not feel

Very Good.

My initial excitement about our move was quickly extinguished, and about a month into our new lifestyle, I was shattered. The farm work was so demanding that we needed help every day, which meant a constant flow of WWOOFers[1], three to eight of them at a time, living in and around my house.

As much as I loved meeting new people, hearing about their adventures and sharing stories, at heart, I was an introvert, and I preferred social time in small doses.

The lack of privacy and the added weight of attending to others' emotional and living needs was gruelling. On top of that, I had my career as a life coach and workshop facilitator—which was also about paying attention to what others needed. I desperately needed some 'me' time.

One winter morning when Martin was going to be out, I planned to curl up by the fire with a hot cup of tea and quietly meditate, with no one needing anything from me for a whole two hours. Bliss.

That morning was frosty. I could see my breath as I wandered downstairs to snuggle in by the fire, but the downstairs was just as cold as the upstairs—the fire wasn't lit. My smile disappeared. Martin always lit the fire in the mornings. *Why didn't he light it this morning?*

Unlike in our city house, where you pressed a button and, like magic, the gas heater came on, in the country a wood burner was our only source of heat. I

---

[1] WWOOFers are Willing Workers On Organic Farms, although it didn't matter that our farm was not certified organic. They are usually travellers from overseas, who work in exchange for food and accommodation.

rubbed my hands together, attempting to warm myself. My fingers were so cold I could hardly feel them.

I looked in the wood box. Empty. *Maybe that's why he didn't light it. There's no wood inside.* My gaze moved up and out of the window, through the icy rain, into the next paddock, and finally located the woodshed. We had been so busy settling in, that stacking wood by the house hadn't made the to-do list.

I took in a deep breath. *Okay, my day is not going to start like I planned.* Regardless of how I felt about it, there was only one thing to do.

I grabbed my raincoat, pulled on my gumboots and trudged through the rain to the woodshed, towing the little wood wagon behind me. The wind was bitterly cold, and I clutched at the neck of my raincoat, trying to seal the gaps. The woodshed was almost as big as a barn, and there were stacks of wood everywhere. I wondered why there were different stacks. I picked one pile and put as much wood as could fit onto the wagon.

Back at the house, I shook off my wet weather gear and filled up the wood box. Standing there dusting off the last of the dirt from my hands I thought with some satisfaction, *Step One accomplished.* Step Two was another matter.

I hadn't made a fire before. I'd never had to.

How hard can it be?

I crunched up some newspaper and stuffed it into the wood burner along with some small pieces of wood, like I'd seen Martin do. I lit the paper and watched eagerly while it burned, but the wood didn't catch.

No fire.

I stuffed more paper under the pieces of wood and lit it again. All the paper burned.

No fire.

Feeling frustrated but determined to try one more time, I crinkled more paper and added more kindling on top of it.

No fire and lots of smoke.

I opened the windows and looked at the clock. Somehow two hours had passed. The WWOOFers would be coming in for breakfast any minute. Feeling defeated, I hung my head and clung on to my cold mug of tea with my mittened hands. I was too tired to cry.

I felt a tap on my shoulder and turned. It was Emily. "Everything is ready, Leanne. We should probably eat soon." I smiled and reached up to grab her hand, grateful for her support. She had taken care of all the important details, such as making sure there was enough cutlery, plates and cups for everyone—the kind of thing I would have thought about at the last minute.

I'd never had such a big bash before, and everything seemed to be going so smoothly. The bonfire was lit, and people had gathered around it. The trestle tables made from recycled doors had been filled with homemade food from all of the guests. Self-appointed chefs had been busy cooking on barbecues borrowed from neighbours. Everyone had pitched in.

"Wonderful!" I squealed, squeezing Emily's hand. "Let's have a blessing circle!" I said spontaneously, without considering whether that would work with so many people from such different areas of my life. It was too late to change my mind, though. The circle was already taking shape. I imagined some of my neighbours standing with their arms staunchly folded hiding their hands under their armpits, but they didn't. I watched as they awkwardly reached out to hold the hands of the people beside them, and my heart filled with love and compassion.

As the circle formed, everyone fell silent, even the children. Their faces turned to me. For a split second I wondered if my hair looked alright, and my hands reached to fluff it up. Then I forgot about my hair as I took a moment to look into people's eyes around the circle. All I could feel was love.

One person was missing though—Miriam. We had met sixteen years ago at a women's business networking event, and became great friends since then. Over the last few years she spent more and more time travelling around the world with her consulting business. She said she was a 'global citizen,' and each year she returned to New Zealand for Christmas and New Year. She had already left. I was sad she couldn't be there.

Bringing my attention back to the circle, I was still uncertain if I would be heard at the outer reaches, so I spoke as loud and strong as I could. "I am so happy to be here with you all," I said. Finally I could say that and really feel it.

"Thank you to everyone who helped make this day happen. Thanks to our marvellous WWOOFers, who prepared this space for the festivities." It felt wonderful to be singing the WWOOFers' praises and truly meaning it. "And a big thank you to my husband, Martin." My eyes searched the circle for him but I couldn't see him. "And to all of you for being here, for sharing your food, your hearts, your music and your glorious selves. We are truly blessed. Let's eat!"

It all seemed Very Good.

Chapter 2

The morning melody of birdsong reached my ears as I lingered in the delicious state in-between waking and dreaming. Almost a month had gone by since my party, and life had settled into a peaceful routine.

"It's time to leave," I heard a very clear and gentle voice say.

My eyes shot open. "What?" I whispered, not quite conscious enough to grasp if there was someone there. Martin and I had our own bedrooms, at my request. He got up very early and liked to tinker around. I snored, so he didn't get much sleep next to me. And besides, I liked having my own space.

There was no one in the room but me.

I sat upright, fully awake now, my ears alert to any sound. "Time to leave what?"

Silence.

Maybe I'm still dreaming. Did I actually hear a voice? Am I imagining it?

"What am I supposed to leave?" I tried one more time, hoping the voice would speak again, and hoping it would be quiet forever.

Silence.

My heart pounded in my chest. A deep feeling of dread filled my whole being. You see, I knew this voice.

I had heard it before.

When I was a child, I spent hours outside speaking to the trees and the rocks, and they spoke back. They didn't speak like you and me. I heard their words and phrases in my mind and picked up feelings from them that I knew weren't mine. Together, we had deep conversations about life, and in fact I preferred the company of trees and rocks to the company of other children.

When I was in second grade, I sometimes noticed a white light surrounding and following Miss Brown, the teacher. I could see it particularly when the blackboard was behind her. One day I turned to the boy sitting next to me, and asked, "Hey Chris, what's that white thing following Miss Brown?" He looked at me as if I was crazy and turned away. I realised he couldn't see it.

I was seeing the teacher's aura. Everyone has one, and I could see them.

Our house also had ghosts in the attic. How did I know? Well, I used to go up there and talk to them. They didn't talk back, but they made things move. Old newspapers and books shifted and fluttered and sometimes even fell to the floor. At times I watched these events with curiosity, but other times I scared myself silly and raced downstairs screaming.

I soon realised that I could hear, see and sense things that other people couldn't.

My parents had always been very open-minded about spirituality; they never told me that I was being silly or making things up. Instead, they encouraged me to trust my experiences. When I was twelve, they both began to follow their spiritual interests more seriously. My Dad became involved with meditation and practiced daily, and my Mom took classes about intuition and spiritual healing. Curious to find out more about my own experiences, I went along with her.

By the age of thirteen, I was not only participating in but also leading groups of children and adults in meditation and intuition practice. I continued my own training and teaching in this area well into my twenties.

One time, in my mid-twenties, as I was giving a talk about intuition and spirit guides, I looked into the audience and noticed people's eyes glazing over. Maybe that had happened before, but this time my attention focused on it. *They're not listening.* It was one of those fateful moments when I took a small sliver of reality and blew it up to represent my whole world. In that moment, I decided I was on the wrong path and that people weren't interested in hearing about intuition and spirit guides.

I put aside speaking about such things and started up a business delivering corporate workshops on topics like leadership, communication, and motivation— encouraging people to follow their passions even though I had side-lined mine. The days of talking with the rocks and trees and listening to my intuition became forgotten echoes of the past.

I worked very hard. My business did well, and even though I had become quite skilled at playing the charming, confident, gregarious person, inside I was struggling.

After three years in business, I bought my first house in the city. I was living alone. One day, I came home from work, parked my car in the driveway and turned off the motor as usual, but when I tried to open the door, my body wouldn't move. It was as if I was a puppet and all of my strings had been snipped. My limbs were so heavy I couldn't lift them. A crippling emptiness ached in my chest. I wanted so badly to cry, but my eyes only burned dry with tears that wouldn't come.

I felt so desperately sad and I didn't know why. A lone thought wandered in the desert of my being: *Is this all there is to life?*

I sat there for I don't know how long. Gradually, I snapped out of it and some feeling came back to my body. As I got out of the car, an urgent voice in the back of my mind said, "Something important just happened," but I pushed it away.

"Maybe I'll have a glass of wine," I said aloud.

Immediately that voice in my mind, gentle but firm, piped up. "That's right, go unconscious."

I hadn't expected a challenge. *Surely a glass of wine won't hurt. It will help me to relax.*

"And I could get a Thai curry take-away from my favourite restaurant."

The voice confronted me again. "And keep yourself preoccupied by eating."

I stood still for a moment at my front door. The horrible, heavy feeling started to come back again. Then I had what I thought was a great idea.

"I could watch an uplifting movie and make myself feel better!"

But the inner voice responded again. "So you can distract yourself and forget."

As much as part of me wanted to brush the incident aside, clearly another, wiser part was not going to leave me alone until I paid attention. I needed to do something, but what?

I went inside and called Miriam. She suggested I go on a meditation retreat and told me about a charming Buddhist monastery where she had gone. Without giving myself time to change my mind, I found the number for the monastery and called. As I waited for someone to answer, I noticed my hand was shaking. My heart was thudding in my ears.

I had never been to a monastery before. I imagined dark, cold, stone rooms where dour men waved incense and chanted in an eerie droning fashion. I was ready to hang up when someone answered.

"Hello." The soft-spoken male voice was so soothing that all my fear blew away. He told me they had no retreats scheduled. Feeling disappointed, I was about to put the receiver down when a shiver went through me.

"Do you think I could come and stay for a few days anyway?" I asked holding my breath.

Moments of silence passed, and I didn't move for fear of jeopardising what he might say. Then he said, "Sure. We have a small private hut you can stay in." I began breathing again. We arranged for me to stay three nights, over a weekend.

A few days later, a welcome letter came in the mail. It included guidelines for staying at the monastery. "We ask you not to bring items such as makeup, perfume, jewellery, snug or suggestive clothing, musical instruments, electrical appliances..."

I stopped at "electrical appliances." I could go without makeup and wear baggy clothes, but I *needed* my hair dryer. The last time I had let my hair dry naturally was when I was seventeen. Every single morning since then I had used a hair dryer to tame my whispy, wayward curls into shape. My hair usually only looked perfect for about ten minutes before the humidity and wind started to return it to its natural wildness, but all that work was worth it for ten minutes of feeling great. I couldn't imagine leaving the house without it.

It seemed like such a petty thing, and yet not having my hair dryer was a big deal for me. I sighed and put the letter down. There I was, going on a personal retreat to find the reason for my recent feelings of despair, which would probably mean facing some deep, inner fears, and the first fear I would have to overcome would be my own hair.

Chapter 3

The monastery was just outside of the city, tucked into the native bush. The entrance from the street had a simple hand-made wooden sign: Bodhinyanarama Buddhist Monastery. It would have been easy to drive by and not notice it. Grasses and ground-cover plants had been tastefully landscaped in front of a six-foot high hand-crafted wooden fence. The gate was open and as I drove through the entrance, I felt as if I was leaving the world of the bustling city behind me and entering an enchanted land.

A young man with a shaved head came out to greet me.

"Welcome, Leanne," he said, bowing. I reached out to shake his hand, but his hands stayed folded in his light brown robes. I quickly withdrew mine, feeling awkward. I discovered later that the monks were not allowed to touch women.

With no planned public activities, the monks mostly left me alone as they attended to their own work. I spent that afternoon walking around the gardens and unpacking my things. The small wooden hut I had been assigned rested on poles about one metre off the ground. Poking my head in, the small space was totally empty apart from a sleeping mat on the floor, and it was just big enough for me and my knapsack.

I looked around for a light but there wasn't one. *That's right.* I recalled the welcome letter: "We ask you not to bring... electrical appliances..." My mind flashed to the image of my hair dryer left in the cupboard at home. *This must be the reason. The huts don't have electricity. Good thing I brought my flashlight.*

When night came I was excited to crawl into my sleeping bag. I had never slept in a hut before. *What an adventure!*

My excitement soon waned as I struggled to find a comfortable position on the hard sleeping mat. Finally, after about an hour, sleep came to get me.

The next morning my alarm went off at four-thirty. I was to report for cleaning duty at five, my exchange for staying there. *Why did I set the alarm so early? There's so little for me to do to get ready.* I pressed the snooze button and went back to sleep. I didn't have to think about what to wear and there was nothing I could do about my hair.

At five o'clock I walked sheepishly into the big meditation hall wearing clothes that looked like pyjamas, and my hair a mess. A monk I hadn't met greeted me. Without thinking my fingers reached to fluff my hair on the flat spot in the back of my head. He smiling warmly and handed me a rag. "Why don't you help me clean the windows?"

Realising that he couldn't care less what I looked like, I started to relax.

Later in the morning, I was sitting in the garden when another monk came to join me. When I saw him coming, my hand automatically flinched to fluff up my hair, but I stopped myself and grinned at how silly it was.

He asked how I was finding my time at the monastery, and I told him that I was already starting to feel more mindful of things that I might not have been so aware of before, like the simple pleasure of sitting with a hot cup of tea. He told me that he always enjoyed having a cup of tea in the evening before going to bed.

I shook my head and said, "A cup of tea before bed would be nice, but then I'd have to get up in the night to pee, and the toilets are too far away."

"Why don't you do what I do?" he said.

"What's that?"

"I keep an empty bottle beside the bed and use that."

I was stunned. First of all, I couldn't believe that we were having such an intimate conversation, and secondly, the logistics of what he was suggesting would be ridiculous. He must have forgotten he was speaking with a woman.

This was a profound realisation for me. There I was in ugly clothes, my hair all in disarray, and I was okay. I was good enough. I felt completely accepted—not for being good, not for being beautiful, not for being a woman, simply for being a fellow human being. It made me realise how harshly I had been judging myself, and how tired I was of trying so hard.

The monk chuckled as the impracticality of his comment dawned on him, too. "Oh, that wouldn't work for you, would it?" We both laughed.

In the afternoon as I strolled along one of the bush

paths, I reached out to touch the leaves and then quickly withdrew my hand, feeling silly. *What are you doing? You are doing nothing but walking and touching leaves! How frivolous when there is so much real work that needs attending to back in the office!* There was that voice again. So harsh and critical. Never satisfied with me the way I was. Always demanding more.

I went to the kitchen, made myself a cup of tea and sat in the garden amid all the colourful flowers. The harsh voice piped up again. *Shouldn't you be doing something productive?* I got up to walk again, hoping to leave my thoughts behind me, but like annoying flies, they continued to harass me.

I sat down again and closed my eyes. I began to breathe evenly in and evenly out, and my body started to relax. I needed to find that still place inside myself that I once knew, but my mind wasn't going to let me. *You don't have time for this!*

I wasn't yet ready to let go. I still couldn't offer myself the acceptance that the monks had offered me.

Fast forward to ten years later. Martin and I had just married. We had a big house in the city and I was still working hard, still listening to the slave driver in my mind. Everything looked perfect from the outside. But that heavy emptiness opened up again, and this time it was even more bleak.

I shared with Martin how I felt. "Why don't you take some time off," he said. I nodded. That was just what I was thinking. Memories of the monastery flashed into my mind, and I knew I needed to go on a retreat again.

Miriam had introduced me to a woman who owned a couple of small cabins in the woods up the coast, just an hour from our house. She rented the cabins for retreats, and that was just the sanctuary I needed. Luckily one was available. Organising my work to take the Monday off I headed up the coast in the late afternoon on Friday, making it a nice long weekend. I would create my own monastery, and this time I was determined to stay until I had some insight into where my feelings of despair were coming from. I hoped that would be before the end of the weekend.

The next morning, sitting on the cabin porch, I looked out into the bushes waiting for a sign. I wasn't sure how this was going to go. A big, tall oak tree right in front of me caught my attention. My eyes explored it: large branches stretching broadly overhead, thick and weathered bark, and two big holes where branches had been cut off over the years.

It had been a long time since I had spoken with a tree, and I wondered if I remembered how.

Looking at the tree, I held a question in my mind. "What's missing in my life?"

I listened to the gentle breeze through the leaves. No answer. My cheeks flushed with embarrassment. *That is just a game for children.* I was ready to dismiss the exercise. Then I heard a voice. The voice seemed to come from within my mind, but I knew it wasn't me talking, because it said something I wouldn't have said and the tone of the words had a unique quality—deep and slow.

"What do you want?"

It had been so long since I had talked with trees. It felt very soothing, but I was disappointed with what the tree said. Quickly and a little impatiently I replied, "What do you mean? I have everything I could ever want."

Silence.

I reflected. Having done this before, I remembered that trees asked good questions. Answer, I coached myself. *What do I want?* But I didn't know. I sighed. *This is going to take all day!*

I was thinking about getting up and going for a walk when an inkling of awareness opened up and I recognised that I had a habit of avoiding sitting still with myself. I decided to face the tree and myself, and all my inner conflict disappeared.

Holding the tree's question in my mind, I closed my eyes and asked the deepest part of myself: **What** do *I want? What **do** I want? What do **I want**?*

The question sunk into me like a pebble sinking to the bottom of a well. I was so still I could hear the beating of my heart. And then, as if it had bubbled up from that very deep place, I heard a soft and quiet voice answer, "I want to live like this."

I immediately recognised the voice. It was the voice of my heart.

It had been so long since we last spoke, or since I had last listened. I was excited to be in contact again with this deep part of myself, but the message confused me. *What does it mean? Do I want to live in a cabin in the bush?*

I couldn't yet see how this was related to my question about what was missing in my life.

I let myself sit and really feel what my heart just said. "I want to live like this." Like a pot of tea, I let it seep, allowing the true flavours of every leaf, flower and root to release their messages into the water. As the message seeped into me, I realised that I longed to live in nature and take the time for moments of quiet and solitude, just like I was doing then. This desire had been deeply buried under my belief that in order to be good enough I had to work hard and succeed, and that I didn't have time for moments like this.

Other messages came that weekend, from the tree, my heart and my intuition, but none as powerful. Trusting in my heart's answer to the question, I sat on the porch most of that weekend and created plans for a new lifestyle. I was excited, inspired, and knew I was on track.

When I returned to my lovely home in the city with Martin, I immediately set about making the changes I had planned. I arranged to spend more weekends in the cabin, making time to reflect and talk with nature. I began watching documentaries on climate change, resilient communities and permaculture. As my lifestyle altered, a renewed desire for my spiritual work arose and I began offering courses on intuition and meditation again.

I felt alive and had a passion for life that I hadn't felt in a long time. The horrible feelings of despair were no longer there.

Martin and I created a vision of sharing some land with others and living in an intentional community. We bought the almond farm with our vision in mind. There we were surrounded by nature, and even though settling in on the farm had been full of challenges, I had met and overcome all of them. I was in a Very Good place, and I had worked very hard for it.

That morning, when I was still half-asleep, hearing a voice say "It's time to leave" was a total shock, but I recognised it as the voice of my heart. How could my heart now be saying that?

It was so hard to understand. And even harder to understand was that I hadn't heard my heart speaking to me for so long that I had forgotten about it. *Have I been side-tracked? Did I stop listening? And if it is time to leave, then, what am I supposed to leave? My marriage? The farm? My work?*

As I thought through and felt into the possibility of losing all these parts of my life, I was shocked to discover that I was not attached to any of them. For a few fleeting seconds, I considered that I could actually leave it all, even the country. Nothing was holding me here. I felt totally free and even physically lighter.

Then I imagined myself telling Martin, and all my joy and lightness fell heavily to the ground.

I shook my head. *What am I thinking? I don't want to leave. Why would I want to leave? This is crazy.* My mind tried to claw back some ground.

I got dressed and went to the bedroom door. There was work I needed to do. Holding the doorknob, I paused. I didn't want to go out. It felt safer in my room.

I opened the door and stepped into the hall. My whole body tightened with guilt. I knew nothing in that house, nothing in my life, would ever be the same. Everything would be tainted with the knowledge that I had thought of leaving it.

I can't say anything. Who could I tell? Emily? *She won't believe me*. Miriam? *She won't understand. No one will understand*. People would think I'd gone mad, hearing voices telling me to do something that didn't make sense. As I walked downstairs to the kitchen, all I could think about was what I couldn't say.

Chapter 4

I sat alone in the kitchen holding my cup of tea tightly, as if this would help me hold myself together. The ranch slider opened, and Martin walked in. My face flushed. I hadn't even done anything, but I felt so guilty. He headed straight for the office, which was right beside the kitchen, without looking at me.

"How's it going?" I called out.

No answer. *Maybe he didn't hear me.* But his response wasn't unusual. We didn't have much to do with each other in those days. Martin was out by the time I was up, and he spent his days with the WWOOFers and ate most of his meals with them. I spent most of my time in our home office or in the city seeing clients. Neither of us seemed to mind this arrangement, or at least neither of us said anything.

Even our date nights were strained. "Do you want some of my fish?" I asked him as we sat in a restaurant one evening. He shook his head, not lifting his gaze from his plate as he cut into his steak. The restaurant was filling up. I watched the people talking and laughing as the waitress showed them to their tables. *The décor is quite nice in here*—I chewed my dry and tasteless fish—*but I think the food is over-priced.*

I looked at Martin eating. "How's your meal?

"Good," he said, glancing at me for a second. A couple

seated nearby, their heads leaning in towards each other, looked like they were engaged in an enjoyable and intimate conversation. I sighed, feeling lonely.

Turning my attention to Martin again, I asked, "How was your day today?"

"Good," he said. He continued to look at his plate. *How can he sit there and not say anything? What's going on in his mind?*

"Are you ready?" he said as soon as I put the last forkful in my mouth. *So that's it? We're not really going to connect then, are we?*

It hadn't always been that way. Our meeting was like a magical fairy-tale. It seemed we were destined to be together. We talked. We laughed. We cried. He said he loved the food I made. We shared our passions, our hopes, our fears. We talked for hours about the future and the kind of life we could create.

What had changed? Did we marry too soon? We only knew each other eight months on our wedding day, and even though I had already been married, this time I was sure it was different. I felt that he and I could create anything together. What had gone wrong?

"What don't you like about it?" Martin asked the first time we visited the almond farm. *Was that anger or exasperation in his voice?* He rarely showed how he felt, so an expression of feeling, no matter how small, took me by surprise. I always figured it must have been his English upbringing. Immediately I felt guilty, as if I had done something to disappoint him.

We had been looking for almost two years. We hoped

to buy some land with a few other people, but that had fallen through. Miriam and I had talked briefly about her joining us but with her travel schedule it didn't seem a beneficial arrangement. Now Martin and I were looking for property on our own and hoping to attract others to join us. Martin was tired of looking. He loved this property and was keen for us to buy it.

"It feels so busy to me," I said as I looked at the rows and rows and rows of almond trees, all of them straight and even, all pruned and shaped in just the right way. Three thousand trees that would have to be maintained, all busy growing nuts that would have to be harvested and sold. I felt exhausted just looking at them.

"It doesn't feel peaceful here." I felt torn inside, afraid to disappoint him and unwilling to hold back the truth. "I don't want to run a farm. I want to run my intuition courses and work with my clients." I couldn't see how we were going to create the eco-village lifestyle we wanted by buying this property. Besides, Martin also had his own business doing IT consulting and I wondered how he was going to handle that and all the farm work. But he said that didn't bother him.

In the end, the fear of disappointing Martin overrode what I knew deep down was right for me, and I agreed to go ahead. When our offer went unconditional, I felt sick. Panicked, I asked Martin if we could pull out, knowing we would have to pay a penalty, but he refused, and I caved in. The farm was ours.

Before long, we had a house full of WWOOFers and there was much, much more work than I could ever have anticipated. I tried desperately to create a home that supported me and to address my needs, but Martin and I argued about everything, from painting the walls to putting in a closet so I could hang my clothes, to letting some of the land grow wild.

I had expected the changes in lifestyle to be challenging, but I hadn't expected my biggest challenges would be with Martin.

One rare morning, Martin hadn't gone out early and we were both in the kitchen. His arms were folded over his big chest as his one-point-nine metre heavy frame leaned against the kitchen bench. "Can we talk?" I asked. I wanted to talk with him about how unhappy I was having all of the WWOOFers in the house and to discuss what we could do about it. I wanted to know how he was feeling living here and how things were going for him. Basically, I just wanted to connect.

"Sure," he said. I started to get excited. We were actually going to have a conversation! Since we had moved onto the farm, we hadn't been speaking with each other very often. Maybe we were just too tired. Maybe we didn't have anything to say. Maybe we had so much to say we didn't know where to start.

"Are you happy here?" I asked. By "here" I meant, on the farm and living this lifestyle, which was so far from the vision I thought we'd had.

"I'm in heaven," he said. Looking out the window, he pointed to a tree in the garden. "I want you to bury my ashes there." Martin had managed to reduce his other business to one day a week in the city and the rest of the time he worked on the farm. That was heaven for him.

No! He can't really mean that. I looked into his eyes, and they were unmoving. He was settled, and that was that. *But I don't want to live here for the rest of my life.* Tears of frustration and helplessness welled up in my eyes.

"What about our vision of sharing land with a group of people and creating community?" I asked, feeling desperate. That was why we had come there. Everything we had been doing had been working towards that.

"That's idealistic," he said. "We have community with the WWOOFers."

I was dumbfounded. Our whole relationship had been about creating that vision, and I couldn't believe he was abandoning it.

"Is your vision fulfilled living like we are right now?" I asked with a very dry mouth, fearing the worst.

He nodded.

Desperate, I blurted out, "Well it isn't for me. I'm not in heaven. This lifestyle is hell for me, and I'm really unhappy." *Please listen to me. Please let's talk about this.*

Martin got up to leave. "Where are you going?" I asked, panicking. *Is that it? Is that all the talking we're going to do?* "I thought we were going to talk."

Why do I feel like I'm grasping at thin air? Why can't I reach him? Why won't he just sit and speak with me? Why can't we work this out together?

He turned and walked out the door without saying another word, and that was when something inside of me switched. I was unwilling to be that unhappy. If he wasn't going to work with me, then I was going to take charge of doing what I needed to do to make myself happy. I would no longer ask for his partnership, his permission or his help.

Very quickly I made some big changes. I declared our house a private space, where no one was allowed to come unless they were invited. We had a self-contained cottage an acre away, and I set that up so the WWOOFers could prepare their own meals, sleep and hang out there. Martin and I had a joint account into which each of our business accounts contributed. I took some money from my business account and some from our joint account and bought a kit-set small cabin. With the help of a builder, I created a magical place for my meditation and my work. I also had a closet built in my bedroom, and in exchange for some coaching sessions, I had a few walls painted.

It was interesting that Martin stopped fighting me when I made it clear I was going ahead with these alterations regardless of what he said. I felt sad that it took me having to go against him to make those things happen, but on the other hand I knew that it wasn't up to Martin to take care of my needs. That was my job. What he thought about all the changes, I didn't know. He didn't say and I didn't ask.

I felt so much more settled having my own working space, a bit more order and a home where I could walk around in my dressing gown without wondering who was going to come in at any given moment. It was just what I needed.

My big birthday party came on the heels of these new things, and I was feeling like I'd accomplished a lot.

But then the voice came and put an end to all my new feelings of security.

As I sat drinking my lukewarm tea, sitting in the kitchen and staring blankly out the window at nothing, I tried again to convince myself that everything was okay. *It isn't that bad with Martin really. We've gone through a lot together. Our skills are complementary. We share common interests. What more could I want?*

What more could I want? That last thought repeated itself in my mind. I got up and washed my cup.

A few days later, I was walking through the bush alone. The ground felt soothing to step on as I followed the meandering path. Feeling my arms sway by my side, I took in some nice belly breaths as I contemplated my circumstances again. *Maybe hearing this voice say, "It's time to leave" is a symptom of a mid-life crisis? I have just turned fifty. Maybe something got triggered inside that is luring me to do wild and outrageous things?*

Or maybe this is a calling? A calling to something higher or a calling to simply guide me elsewhere?

I felt myself drawn to stray from the path. Usually I didn't wander off the track unless I knew an area well, but when I saw an overgrown side-track, one that would easily be missed, I stepped onto it, and it led me to a river I didn't know was there.

As I watched the river trickling through the stones my heart felt uplifted and soothed. I breathed in the image and the sounds, and decided to talk to the river. Kneeling down to touch the cool water, I asked it, "What is a calling?"

As I watched the water flowing freely, I received its message. "A calling is the flow of spirit encouraging you to go one way, or to go another way."

That is what happened when I felt drawn to walk down this path.

Observing the river again, I saw how it flowed effortlessly. Some areas were quicker, other areas slower. It flowed around and over rocks. In other places it had stopped and pooled, but only for a time, because the flow changed moment by moment, day by day.

What if I don't follow the flow? What if this is a calling and I don't listen?

Not knowing how to deal with my situation, I decided to get some professional guidance.

Isobelle worked from her home, which was high on a hill with the most spectacular views of the sea. As I climbed the stairs to her house, each step bringing me closer to her door, I felt more and more anxious, and my stomach tightened. I was both afraid and excited about what I might find out.

Her warm hug and smile relieved some of my tension. She was a therapist, but she was also a friend, and I trusted her completely.

"Relax, Leanne," she said as I lay on the couch. *Relax? How can I relax? My whole life is at stake!* I took a deep breath and let it out slowly, tightly gripping the edges of the couch cushion.

In this session Isobelle would use hypnosis. She would guide me to a very deep state of inner awareness, also called the Higher Self.

Her soft voice soothed me. I closed my eyes and slowly my fingers loosened their grip. The muscles in my arms and shoulders softened. My belly relaxed and my back began to melt into the cushions supporting me. A familiar peaceful heaviness descended through my whole body.

I was deeply relaxed and conscious at the same time. Isobelle's voice seemed like an echo in the background as if coming from a tunnel. She told me she was going to ask me the questions I had prepared before coming to the session. My Higher Self would be answering them.

As she asked the questions, I heard myself speak, but I was not in control of my speaking. Words were coming out of my mouth, but my voice was deeper than usual, and I listened as if I was a bystander listening to two people having a conversation. It was fascinating.

Isobelle asked, "What do you have to say about the voice Leanne heard the other morning that said, "It's time to leave?" I was all ears. How would this wise and all-knowing part of me respond?

Without missing a beat, I heard my Higher Self say, "She no longer has desire to be in a relationship." My body stiffened with fear. I felt like a child who had eavesdropped on her parents and accidentally heard them reveal some secret that jolted her world.

Isobelle continued to question, "What do you mean, 'she no longer has desire to be in a relationship'? Do you mean with Martin or with anyone?"

"Both. She doesn't need and she doesn't desire to be in a relationship," the deep voice within me responded.

They kept talking back and forth, Isobelle asking questions and my Higher Self responding, but I didn't remember what else they said. My conscious mind became consumed with what it had just heard.

No need and no desire to be in a relationship. That was a lot to digest. And as I checked in with my heart, my head, my gut and my toes for verification, each time the answer was yes. It was true.

When the session was over, I was too shocked to speak. We sat there for some time in silence. She let me talk first. "I'm going to just let this sink in," I said as I got up to leave.

She gave me a big hug. "Are you going to tell Martin?" I shrugged. I'd only just told myself.

She smiled the most compassionate of smiles.

As I left Isobelle's house, I struggled to keep my balance walking down the stairs. Feelings of terror and exhilaration pulsated through my body. It was exhilarating to know the truth and terrifying to think about the consequences.

Chapter 5

I decided to speak with another professional, to see if that would help me to process what I had just learned. Randall was a wise, very intuitive, not-shy-to-ask-the-tough-questions kind of counsellor. I thought maybe getting a male's perspective on this whole situation might shed some different light. Maybe he would give me a different message, a message confirming that this was a mid-life crisis after all, and that all I would need to do was to wait for a little time to pass. I was also hoping that further counselling would help me to decide what to do next.

The first thing he did was to clarify that nothing was wrong. Nothing was wrong with the farm, with Martin or with me. Everyone and everything was doing what they were supposed to do and they were not wrong for that. When my mind opened to the truth of this, I actually felt love for Martin again. It was so nice not to be resisting him for once.

The next thing Randall did was to confirm what I was afraid was true—that I didn't want to be in a relationship with Martin any more. I still felt love for him, but I had no desire to be with him.

It was both petrifying and helpful to have Randall confirm what I already knew, but it was up to me to do the hard work of taking the next step. Isobelle's words echoed in my mind, "Are you going to tell Martin?" *Am*

I? I started to feel sick again. *WHAT exactly will I say? "So Martin, guess what happened to me the other morning? I heard this voice telling me to leave, so I went to see a hypnotist and an intuitive counsellor who both confirmed that I should leave you, and so I wanted you to know that I'm leaving. I hope you'll understand."*

Later that evening while Martin was having dinner with the WWOOFers at their cottage, I sat by myself on the couch. I thought about one of the techniques that I used with my clients when they were challenged with making a decision, and I decided to use it on myself. The technique had two parts.

Part One: In my mind, I pretended that I had decided to leave Martin and then I observed my reaction.

I felt totally calm and at peace. My heart was wide open, and all I could feel was love. Tears flowed down my cheeks as I reminisced about the good times we had shared. I envisaged him sitting at the table with the WWOOFers, laughing and relaxing after a long day. "I'm going to leave you," I whispered, and I cried harder, feeling so sad but also so relieved.

I closed my eyes and visualised telling my friends. My vision unfolded like this:

> *I gathered a group of friends and told them Martin and I were separating.*
>
> *Their eyes opened wide with shock and disbelief. "You're what?!" they shouted, not with care and concern, but with anger and disapproval. "No! You're kidding? What are you doing that for? Oh my God! What's wrong?"*

Among my friends, I saw Emily's angry face as she was shaking her finger at me, and Miriam was standing there with her arms folded looking at me detached. A pain stabbed in my heart.

They were like a pack of wolves turning on me. I was hurt and terrified, but I understood their shock and anger. I hadn't shared with any of them about my struggles with Martin and the farm, not to mention the voice and the therapy sessions. I had been too busy dealing with my life to talk about it. I also feared if I gave voice to my problems, I would make them bigger.

So no one knew, not even Miriam and Emily. How could they possibly understand?

I wanted to lash out and tell them everything that was wrong with Martin and our relationship, but I knew that wouldn't go very well. My mind rummaged through its filing cabinets for one big juicy reason why I was leaving, something that would satisfy everyone.

"We grew apart," I said meekly, finding nothing else to say.

Their eyes narrowed and grew dark. "How could you leave him after all you've been through? How could you walk away? You're leaving another marriage! I don't believe this! I'm disgusted with you! How could you let him down?" Their snarls trailed off as they turned their backs to me and walked away.

I opened my eyes. My hands were trembling. I knew that my vision wasn't real, but that didn't stop me from feeling sick in the pit of my stomach.

When I was a child I use to have a recurring dream in which all my friends and family became werewolves and turned against me. Often I woke up in a cold sweat, unable and unwilling to go back to sleep for fear I would fall back into the nightmare.

Even though the nightmare was long gone, the fear of people turning against me was still paralyzing.

"I can't do this. I can't leave. I have to stay," I whispered, and I felt a bit of relief.

I also reminded myself that this was just a technique.

Part Two: I imagined myself having decided to stay.

Sitting back I tried to relax but something wouldn't let me. I closed my eyes again and new images flickered through my mind. This time I saw:

> *The farm with a lone figure in the distance. I knew it was me. It was a glimpse of the not-too-distant future. Everything looked the same except the colours were faded, just like my eyes. The vision zoomed in on my face. My eyes were dark and sunken. My skin was grey and had aged. My face had hardened.*

I cringed looking at myself but I was too curious to open my eyes and lose the vision, so I kept my eyes closed and continued watching. The rest of the scene was even more distressing.

> *Others were on the farm working, laughing and*

> *talking together but they all avoided me. If they
> did come near me they became cold and distant.
> Martin was there too. We were visibly miserable
> with each other.*

As I watched the scene I thought, *No one would question
us separating now.*

The vision ended and I opened my eyes. I sat
unmoving in the dead silence of the room.

I felt like a zombie. In just twenty minutes I had gone
from feeling free and peaceful to feeling terrified, bitter,
sad and now deeply disturbed. I had hoped that the
clarity I got from my sessions with Isobelle and Randall
would make things easier, but things were only getting
harder. It looked like no matter what I chose, it was
going to be bad.

I tried to negotiate with myself. *I can just wait and
let time go by. Maybe all of this will blow over and it won't
be such a big deal in the end? Or maybe I can wait until it
becomes so obvious to everyone that it isn't working between
Martin and me?*

This agonising turmoil was familiar. Memories
from the past came to my mind. I remembered Paul, a
boyfriend from my early twenties. He was the love of my
life. We had been living together in bliss for almost three
years. When I was offered a promotion at work, I could
hardly wait to get home and tell him the news. "They've
offered me a management role," I said, my eyes bright
and sparkling with confidence at twenty-four years old.

Paul looked up from his book. There was no smile on
his face. "That will mean you'll be working evenings."

"Yes."

"If you work in the evenings, we are through."

My mouth shut. I blinked a few times and swallowed hard as I tried to take in what I'd heard. My first thought was, *How dare he? This is important to me.* But soon other thoughts overrode my outrage. *Who am I to think I could do whatever I wanted? How thoughtless. How careless. And imagine I could have even ruined my relationship with Paul because of it. It's a good thing I just realised that now. Paul loves me and he wants to spend time with me. That's important in a relationship. He's right. We wouldn't see each other that much anymore if I worked in the evenings. What was I thinking?*

I turned the job down.

Six months later, my relationship with Paul ended anyway.

More memories flooded in.

When I was forty-two, the brother of a friend came to visit from America. James was good looking, very affectionate, and quickly stole my heart. We got along easily and he decided to move to New Zealand so that he would be closer to his brother and we could explore being in relationship.

We spent two months together, then James went back to America to make arrangements for his move. As the weeks and months went by, his conversation gradually changed from, "When I come to New Zealand", to, "If I come to New Zealand", to, "Maybe one day I might come to New Zealand."

As his conversation changed, mine did, too. "When

you come to New Zealand" became, "Hopefully you will come to New Zealand" and then, "Maybe I might move to America." I was getting more and more anxious about losing my relationship with James. One day I sat on the couch to meditate. I closed my eyes, went into a deep state of relaxation, and held the question, "Why do I feel so much turmoil?" I wanted to be in relationship with him but I didn't really want to move to America.

A wise voice from deep within me replied, "Because you are trying to make yourself do something that doesn't feel right to you."

James and I talked about it and agreed to let the relationship go.

More memories flooded in.

The job I hated but stayed at for as long as I could bear it because I didn't want to lose the money; the abusive friendship I kept because I was afraid of being disliked; the painful situation I stayed in because I was afraid of losing face; the unhealthy relationship I hung on to because I was afraid of losing love.

I had compromised myself so many times, and each time I was trying to hang on to something I was afraid of losing. But the moment I compromised, I lost anyway. I lost my heart. I lost my spirit. I lost trust. I lost myself.

I looked out of the window and in the distance saw the lights from the WWOOFer cottage.

Do I stay? Do I go?

Rumi, a famous fourteenth century poet wrote:

"The truth stands before me. On my left is a

blazing fire, and on my right, a cool flowing stream. One group of people walk toward the fire, into the fire, and the other [group] towards the cool flowing waters. No one knows which is blessed and which is not. But just as someone enters the fire, that head bobs up from the water, and just as a head sinks into the water, that face appears in the fire."

The message I got from this was if you faced your fears and dealt with what looked to be more challenging, then what followed would be easier. But if you avoided your fears, taking what looked to be an easier path, your fears only awaited you around the corner.

Sitting there on the couch, I took a deep breath and chose my path.

I chose to leave Martin.

All of my distress fell away. I felt calm. I felt clear. I knew I was doing the right thing.

My first job was to face the fear of what I had seen in my vision. I had no evidence that people would judge me, but whether they were going to or not I wanted to face my fear powerfully. I coached myself as I would coach my client, and I decided to re-enact the vision and to take charge.

I closed my eyes and brought back the images of my friends judging me and turning away from me. Breathing deeply into the centre of my chest, I felt myself become stronger inside. I didn't want to defend or justify myself, and I didn't want to feel like a victim and beat myself up. As I watched them get angry and shout at me, I listened to what they said and realised that a lot of it was true. I was breaking my commitment, and Martin would feel hurt.

In the vision I saw myself speaking to them. "Yes, you are right. I am sorry you have become involved. I know it's hard to understand." I felt compassion as I faced them, feeling peaceful and strong, with nothing more to say.

I imagined myself as an aikido master standing face to face with my opponent—my fear. My feet were planted, knees flexed, right arm out, my fingers flexing back and forth indicating, "I'm ready."

And then I stepped into the fire.

Chapter 6

The next morning I got up a little earlier than usual and completed all of my morning chores and the pressing household management tasks for the week such as bulk food ordering, and WWOOFer communications and bookings. The wall clock in the kitchen said nine forty-five—Martin would come in from the farm soon. I made myself a cup of tea and sat down to wait for him.

I hadn't planned anything. All I knew was that I had to say something and I had to do it now. I felt courage and clarity.

The kitchen was quiet apart from the Very Good bird singing outside the window. I took that as a good omen.

Nine forty-seven. The waiting was agonising. I tried to stay present, but my thoughts were not helping. *What if I don't know what to say? What if I chicken out? What if Martin doesn't come in till later? What if he does come in and he has someone with him? What if the phone rings? What if it all comes out wrong, and we end up fighting?*

The familiar sound of the ranch slider opening pulled me out of my thoughts. Martin walked in. My mind went blank.

Something pushed me out of my chair, and I walked over to greet him. He was heading towards the office as he usually did, but I didn't want to have this conversation in a small, confined space. The thudding in my heart had moved up to my throat, and I whispered, "God, help me." *Keep moving. Keep moving.*

I held my breath, bracing myself, and when I looked into his face a rush of fear flooded my mind. *Speak now!* I commanded myself inside, cutting through the fear. *And breathe, breathe into the centre of your chest.*

Finally I managed to get some words out of my dry parched mouth. "Martin, can we talk about something?"

"Sure," he said. I pointed to the couch for us to sit down.

Inside my mind I continued to coach myself, *Okay, Leanne, this is it. Open your mouth, girl. You can do it.* I looked into his eyes. I had made a promise to myself that no matter what happened, or what he said, I would not become defensive or blame either of us. I was determined that this would not be an argument. I wanted my words to be authentic and to come from my heart. Again, I silently asked for help from the loving divine power of all that is.

He looked at me expectantly. My heart was now pounding in my ears and I kept eye contact with him as these words came out of my mouth: "I don't want to be in a relationship anymore."

There was no sense in beating around the bush, and besides, saying anything else would have led me to justifying and defending. I took a deep, conscious breath. The first, hardest step was now taken. Just like when I went skydiving, jumping out of the plane was the hardest part. After that, there was no going back.

I had just uttered words that would change both of our lives forever.

His face looked strained and shocked. Even though I had tried countless times to talk to him about how I was feeling, the truth was that we really didn't know what was going on in each other's worlds, and this came as a complete surprise to him.

"What did you say?" he asked, probably hoping he'd misheard me. I repeated the same words, reminding myself to keep breathing evenly and deeply.

"You're breaking your vows!" he shouted, shaking his finger at me. The tension rose in my body, and I felt the urge to defend myself. A list of the things that were wrong and reasons why I didn't want to be in a relationship anymore quickly came to my mind, but I said nothing.

Instead I paused. I kept breathing.

We had written our own marriage vows. They were about loving each other with integrity and honesty. As far as I was concerned, I wasn't breaking those vows. In fact, I was being guided by them. But it wasn't worth pointing that out. It would have ended in an argument.

I guessed that he was referring to the implied vow that we were committing to our marriage for the rest of our lives. That had been the intention for both of us when we got married, even though we hadn't explicitly said it, and in that sense what he was saying was true. I was breaking that vow.

Holding his gaze steadily I said, "Yes, I am."

Martin tried to find out what was wrong. Had I met someone? Had he done something wrong? My heart ached for the pain he must have been feeling as he tried desperately to understand.

Our conversation didn't last long. When he left the house, everything went still. My heart had returned to its place in my chest, no longer pumping in my ears. But the stillness was eerie, as if something had died. And something had. The life we had been planning to live had died. Nothing had physically changed, and yet everything around me looked different. Soon this would no longer be my home. Realising this, I felt great relief.

My body was shaking, but I felt good. I knew I had made the right choice.

Chapter 7

My fingers shook as I wrote the note. "I'll be back on Friday."

I had already handled the urgent household matters, and I rescheduled my clients for the week. Throwing a few items of clothing into a bag, I headed off to the little cabin in the bush where I had been before. For four days I collapsed, spending most of my time sleeping and meditating. I was totally worn out, but the time was blissful. Not once did I question my decision to leave.

All too quickly, Friday arrived, and it was time to return to the farm. When I carried my little bag to the car, it felt surprisingly heavy, and I took this as a reflection of my dread of facing Martin when all I wanted to do was run away.

Rumi's poem came to my mind, and I felt some courage again.

When I walked into the house, I summoned up all the bravery I could muster. I can do this, I told myself. Martin was in the office, and I headed straight there.

He looked up from his desk, and with no expression on his face he said, "You're not going to leave just before the harvest are you?"

My breath caught in my throat. I didn't know what I was expecting, but I wasn't expecting that. What did he mean? Was he trying to get me to stay longer so that he could have a chance to change my mind? Or was he trying to make me feel bad for leaving him just before the busiest time on the farm?

Old unhelpful thoughts came flooding back. *How can I be so thoughtless? This is going to be hard enough on him as it is. It would be a terrible thing for me to leave him at this time.*

My courage disappeared as I plunged into guilt. It wasn't just about the timing of my leaving. It was bigger than that. I had failed in my marriage. I had told myself and others that this marriage would last, and I really thought it would, but here I was leaving, and I felt so ashamed.

All I wanted to do was to make Martin feel better— not to help him, but to help myself, to ease my guilt. Then I had an insane thought. *If I stay longer to help him, maybe I can redeem myself? Maybe he might understand that I still care even though I don't want to be in a relationship.*

I agreed to stay for two more months.

Things started off okay. Martin and I agreed not to tell anyone about our separation for the time being except one or two people we thought needed to know, so, on the surface it appeared like nothing had changed. I thought about contacting Miriam and Emily, but I wasn't quite ready yet to deal with other people's responses. I needed more time to get used to the idea myself.

On a day-to-day basis, Martin and I were cooperating with each other. I had my roles and he had his, and things were relatively easy. I thought maybe we could be friends and help each other through our heartache, and there were even moments when I felt sad and almost regretted my decision to leave. But the peace between us was short-lived.

One evening as I walked by the WWOOFer cottage to collect the mail, one of the WWOOFers said to me, "Aren't you going to Emily's for dinner?"

"No. Why?"

"Oh, Martin has already gone there, and I thought you might be going, too."

An icy chill went through my body. *Why wasn't I invited? Why hasn't Emily called me? She must know we are separating.* I could feel it in my bones that something was wrong.

This was only the beginning.

When I got back to the house, I checked my personal emails to see if there was an invitation from Emily that I had missed. But there was nothing. Later that evening the phone rang. It was a friend I hadn't been in touch with for a couple of years. She said she was sorry to hear that Martin and I were separating. When I asked her how she knew, I discovered that right after Martin and I had promised to not say anything to others, he had sent emails to about forty of my friends to tell them I was leaving the marriage and to ask them to help him understand why.

I was furious, and waited up for him to come home. When I confronted him that night, to my horror he told me that he had actually been *meeting* with my friends— not only with Emily and her husband, but with others, as well—to talk about me. I asked him for details, but he wouldn't tell me anything.

My fury turned to shock. I was shocked that Martin had done this. But then as I took it all in, I was even more shocked that no one who had met with Martin, or who had spoken with him, had contacted me. *If they know we're separating, why haven't they called me? Why haven't I heard from any of them?*

Now I didn't know who I could call. Would they be there for me or would they be there for Martin?

Miriam was in Europe. I wondered if Martin had been in contact with her, but I didn't have to wonder for long. I found out she and Martin had been Skyping, and saw the warm and caring hearts and kisses in the chat window they had sent each other.

When I emailed her to tell her how horrible things were, her response was short and detached: "We make choices and our choices have impacts." There was no compassion and there were no love hearts or kisses to me.

My worst nightmares were coming true.

Usually I loved going to bed and peacefully drifting off to sleep. But at that time, the night became a theatre for my mind to replay the horrors of the day over and over and over again. Sleep eluded me, and I couldn't decide which was worse: the daytime and the reality of the bad dream unfolding or the night time, when I was left alone to relive it. Relief was nowhere.

I thought of leaving right away, but I still had six more weeks, and I couldn't break my word yet again. In some horrible way, I felt I deserved what Martin had done. I was such a bad person for hurting him and disappointing our friends and family.

A few days after confronting Martin, I stood with my hand poised above the phone. I imagined Emily picking it up and her voice becoming cold and disconnected when she found it was me calling. I pulled my hand away. *Why hasn't she called me? Doesn't she want to know how I'm feeling?* I could only assume that she had sided with Martin, and that hurt more than anything else.

You can never know in advance what will happen when a marriage breaks up, or how little control you will have over any of it. Some people took sides. Some people changed sides. Some people stepped away, just like in my childhood nightmares. Wisely or unwisely, I stepped back and waited for my friends to contact me rather than contacting them. As a result this was one of the loneliest times in my life.

"Where are you off to?" I asked one afternoon when I walked into the office and saw Martin packing his carry bag. I was trying to keep our interactions as convivial as possible.

"None of your business."

That hurt. "Are you coming back today? Tomorrow?" There was the farm to manage and if queries came in I needed to be able to reach him.

Martin lifted his bag and walked out.

The air between us was cold and we mostly avoided each other apart from discussing details of our settlement.

We agreed on one thing: not to get lawyers involved. We would try to sort out the details ourselves. It didn't go well at first. After a number of hurtful conversations, and no resolution in sight, I came up with a proposal that allowed Martin to keep the farm, his business and other investments, and gave me enough money to support myself for six months and put a deposit on a house. It was important to me that Martin kept the farm, as he loved it there, and that he didn't suffer financially. Maybe this was partly to appease the guilt I still felt.

Martin agreed reluctantly, even though he'd get well over three-quarters of all our assets. We agreed to settle everything before I left the farm, except for the divorce papers which couldn't be filed for another two years.

My struggle at that time wasn't only emotional stress. It was also physical. As the weeks went by my shoulders began to ache, and I couldn't move my arms without searing pain. The physiotherapist said the tendons around my shoulder sockets were inflamed. Then one morning, after a month had gone by, I awoke to find I couldn't move at all. I tried to roll to one side and then to the other, but the pain in my back was too intense. I lay there helpless for two hours before I was able to get myself up.

I hobbled around throughout the following days and weeks, managing to do my work without moving my arms too much or compromising my back. The pain got worse when I sat still, so I kept myself moving as much as I could. Sitting still, however, was unavoidable while teaching my meditation courses.

One time at the end of the two hours, the pain was so bad I was unable to get up out of my chair. I was horrified to have to ask for help but I had to. "Stephen," I said reaching out to a participant. "Would you please help me out of my chair?"

One morning, as I lay in bed feeling sorry for myself, I did the one thing I hadn't thought of doing yet. I asked for help. Closing my eyes, I whispered, "Dear God and all of my angels and all other divine beings on high, please come near me. I need your help."

A soothing calm surrounded me. I breathed peacefully and felt like I was being held. I had been so lost in my own terror that I had forgotten I wasn't alone.

With my eyes still closed, I was shown this vision:

An earthquake was churning beneath my feet. I desperately tried to hold on, but as all of the pieces of my world fell away, nothing remained stable. I cried, I felt hurt, I got angry, I cried some more, I was petrified. But bit by bit, I stopped grasping to hold on. I paid attention to my feet as they found balance in a moving world. I began to feel freer. I let go.

Eventually, the shaking stopped and everything was still. I looked around, afraid I would find my world had been destroyed and there would be nothing left. But as my eyes scanned the space around me, I saw that it was full of new things. A new horizon was there before me, and the sun was beginning to rise.

I opened my eyes and looked outside. The sun was shining. It was a beautiful day. I felt peaceful, really peaceful, for the first time in a long time, and I heard the Very Good bird chirping in the garden.

As each day passed I felt a little stronger. Each time I refused to hold on to hurt, anger, resentment and blame,

I felt a little freer. Things seemed to be a little easier to cope with.

The days and weeks went by and new friends unexpectedly came into my life, like the new landscape in my earthquake vision. My time on the farm was almost finished, with one more week to go.

The worst was over.

Chapter 8

The phone rang, and I eagerly reached for it still hoping it might be Emily, completely forgetting about my shoulders. I winced with the burning pain as I lifted the receiver to my ear.

It was my friend Rebecca. She'd been away and had only just received Martin's email about our separation. "Leanne, are you okay?" Her voice was filled with compassion and concern.

We met in a downtown café. I hadn't seen her since my birthday party, which felt like a lifetime ago, even though it had only been three months. When I arrived at the café, she stood with her arms out, and I felt I was being rescued from being stranded after a great storm in the middle of the ocean with nothing but a life jacket. After weeks of barely hanging on in the water, help had finally arrived. The instant we hugged I began to sob uncontrollably, my relief was so great.

This was the first time I shared the whole story with anyone.

"What are you going to do now?" Rebecca asked. Even though I needed to find a new place to live, I didn't really know what was next. I could buy another house or I could rent something. I could flat with friends. I could go back into the city or I could stay in the country. I could even go back to Canada. There were so many options, but nothing was clear yet.

"I feel like the me I am now isn't capable of making that decision," I said. I didn't mean that I didn't feel well enough or clear enough, I meant that I wasn't enough. "I need to be a bigger me." I needed to see my life from a more elevated, expanded perspective. I needed a transformation in myself.

"How will you do that?"

"I'm not sure. I could go traveling." I knew I needed something to shift my current perspective on my life, and going to different places might do that.

"Oh, that would be exciting. Where would you go?"

"I guess I could go anywhere." I thought about travelling to different countries, but nothing immediately stood out.

"Would you go for a holiday and stay somewhere? Or would you travel around?"

I laughed. "Maybe it isn't so much about going on a holiday somewhere to relax and hang out. Maybe it's more about going somewhere with a purpose or somewhere where there is a special event happening." I could feel my mind churning.

"If I was your client, and I was in the same position you're in, what would you tell me?"

Good question. I took a while to ponder it. "I guess apart from a few coaching sessions, I would recommend that you take one of my courses, which would hopefully create a positive shift in your beliefs about yourself and the world."

"So maybe you should do a course," Rebecca said.

I immediately remembered a documentary about a course called The Shadow Process, which Debbie Ford delivered in the United States. Watching the documentary, I'd felt a strong urge to attend that course, which consisted of a weekend of lectures and exercises about uncovering your own inner darkness and making peace with it.

Rebecca listened intently while I told her what I was thinking. There was one moment from the documentary that especially resonated with me, when Debbie Ford said, "The parts of yourself you are not yet at peace with will undermine your dreams."

Rebecca grabbed my hand and said, "I want to come with you!" She had two young girls, her husband wasn't well, and she was the family's sole breadwinner, so I suspected she wouldn't really come, but her excitement affirmed my own.

Then I remembered having received an email advertising an event in Glastonbury, England. The Prophet's Conference was a five-day gathering of people from around the world with well-known experts speaking on topics ranging from climate change and the Mayan calendar to crop circles and the transformation of human consciousness. The conference would be followed by one week of guided tours to sacred sites in the area. I had read every detail of the advert and then tucked it away, never dreaming that I would be able to go.

I told Rebecca about the conference. "Infinite possibilities! What other ideas do you have? You might as well give yourself lots of options," she said.

There was one other journey that immediately came to mind. I had always wanted to go to Arizona, and I couldn't think of a better way to visit that place than by going on a vision quest guided by a shaman. Shamanic practices were already a part of my life and my teachings, and putting myself in training with someone would be very enriching.

Each of these adventures would be abundant in opportunities for personal development. But which one would be best suited for me? *Which one will deliver the best outcome?* I sat back in my chair. "I don't know which one to choose. Maybe I have too many ideas now."

My excitement waned a little as I thought through the potential costs involved and the amount of time away from my work that any one of these ventures would require. Now that I needed to support myself financially on my own again, I needed to earn more money, particularly if I was going to pay a mortgage. *This isn't a good time to go on a holiday.*

Rebecca stayed silent a few moments and then, as if she was reading my thoughts, she said, "What would you do if time and money were not an issue?"

The question landed inside my head like an arrow hitting the bulls-eye. My mouth opened as if to speak and then closed. *What would I do if time and money were not an issue?* I stopped trying to figure out which one would best fit my circumstances, and I looked down at my hands. I knew what I would do. My heart started to beat louder, like a drum beat calling me to something bigger.

I would do it all. The only question left was—how?

We'd been talking for more than two hours, and it was time to go. "Call me anytime." Hearing the love and warmth in Rebecca's voice, my heart almost burst with gratitude. As I walked down the street, my feet barely touched the ground. I sensed I was about to embark on a powerful adventure that was going to alter me.

Once I had made my decision, things fell into place effortlessly. The whole journey would take just over two months. This wasn't too long a time-frame to risk losing clients, in fact they were supportive and inspired, and they looked forward to hearing about my adventures when I returned. To cover the cost of my trip, I decided to give myself a limited budget from the separation settlement and then trust that everything would work out.

Flights, places to stay and registration for events were arranged with ease.

I would spend the first two weeks in Glastonbury, England, attending The Prophet's Conference and touring sacred sites in the area. After that, I left two weeks of unplanned time to follow my intuition and integrate some of what I had learned.

The second part of my journey would begin with The Shadow Process, a weekend course, at New York's Omega Institute. After that I'd spend three weeks in Arizona including a six-day shamanic vision quest in Sedona. Finally, the last two weeks of my pilgrimage I would visit with my Mom in Ontario, Canada, before returning home to New Zealand.

The whole adventure was perfectly designed just for me and each part of it was a necessary component. The anticipation of my journey and all the planning helped me to get through my last week on the farm.

On the last two weekends, dear women friends— some old, who Martin had not contacted, and some new—came to help me pack. They reached up and crouched down, pulling things out of cupboards that I couldn't reach because of my shoulder and back pain. Together we carefully wrapped and boxed every item I owned. We talked. We laughed. We shared. It was nurturing and uplifting.

Finally it was time to leave. After more effort than I ever thought possible, two months were over. I had kept the large household running with all of the WWOOFers and had helped out with the harvest. My job was done. The moving truck was packed with my stuff ready to go to the storage unit, my car was filled with everything I needed for one more month in New Zealand and two months travelling.

I had already said my farewells to the chickens. I cried as I told the hen-pecked one she'd have to fend for herself now. I had already walked the land and thanked my special places for their care of me: the grove of trees where I loved to have my outdoor shower; my meditation cabin nestled in the bush where I did all of my work; and the rows and rows of trees and multiple garden beds that had fed me.

My last goodbye was to Martin.

I had spent most of my time avoiding him, but this

was the final moment, and I couldn't just leave without saying anything. I was about to go and look for him when he unexpectedly came around the side of the house. "I thought you were gone," he said coolly.

Tears welled in my eyes. *No, don't cry! I don't want to cry.* I had been falling apart for two months with him, and I wanted to at least be able to say goodbye without being an emotional mess.

In spite of all the hurt we caused each other, I still really cared. There was a part of me that didn't want to care, but clearly it was being overruled, because I did. I cared how he felt, and I cared what happened to him.

"I wanted to say goodbye," I said.

An awkward pause rested in the air between us as we stood looking at each other. I half expected him to walk away as he usually did, but he didn't. I took a deep breath and stepped forward to hug him. We hadn't shown any tenderness towards each other in months. I thought he would go rigid, resisting me, but he didn't. As we held each other, I wanted to say how grateful I was for having met him, but I stayed silent.

I took a step back to look into his grey eyes. "Goodbye," I whispered. His face softened from the harsh look I had become accustomed. The wind blew a wisp of his thick curly black hair across his forehead. *He is very handsome.*

"Goodbye," he said softly, with tears in his eyes. *Why couldn't we have been more emotionally available with each other before this moment?*

I turned and walked to my car. I didn't know if he

stood there watching me leave, because I didn't look back. I didn't know if he ever understood why I left.

I carefully climbed into the driver's seat minding my back and shoulders. As I made my way down the long driveway, I waved goodbye to the farm, feeling very peaceful. A gentle drizzle felt comforting on my arm. The cool refreshing wetness touched lightly on my face, and I smiled. I was sure I heard the Very Good bird. "Thank you," I whispered.

I rolled up my window and turned onto the road. My married life had just ended. My life on the farm, after eighteen months, had ended.

A new life had begun.

Chapter 9

Gathering the bed covers around me and propping myself up with some pillows, I reached for the pen and paper, trying not to irritate my shoulder. After a couple of weeks staying in several different places, I was now spending my final two weeks in New Zealand housesitting for a friend. I was grateful to have the space to myself.

During our last counselling session, Randall gave me an assignment. I had been avoiding it, but I promised myself I would do it this morning. Taking a big sigh, I wrote...

Dear Martin,

My pen paused in mid-air. I stared at my first line and read it a few times. *Let's start again, and this time he isn't 'dear.'*

Martin,

My assignment was to write three letters. The first was a letter to Martin telling him everything I wanted to say, unedited, holding nothing back. Next, I was to pretend to be Martin responding to my first letter, writing as I thought he would respond. Finally, I was to be Martin responding to my first letter, but this time writing how I wanted him to respond, saying everything I wanted to hear from him.

What do I really want to say to Martin? I wondered,

fiddling with my pen. I held the pen above the paper again, but my hand wasn't moving. *Surely there must be so much,* but nothing came.

Finally, I wrote a few words.

I wanted to let you know that our marriage break up was really painful for me.

So guarded, so careful. *What do I really feel?* The answer was clear. Nothing.

But how can I feel nothing? Have I really pushed my feelings down so far that I am numb? Maybe. But there is something there, I just don't know how to say it.

I tried again, scratching a few more words on the page, but I quickly crossed them out. *You shouldn't have written that. That's not nice.*

My inner judge was holding the pen. No wonder I couldn't write.

Then another voice inside me, wiser and stronger, stepped forward and said, *It's okay, Leanne. You are not going to send the letter. Go back through the moments of the last few months and write what you felt then.*

As I let my guard down and started to write, very slowly anger began to rise. I wrote a few words, and then a few more, until the anger poured out onto the page like an erupting volcano. I wrote and rewrote the letter again and again, adding more things as they arose. I didn't want to hold on to any of it.

All of the anger, the hurt, the grief spewed out onto the paper. When I had finished, I decided to read the letter out loud to the kitchen cupboards, pretending that the cupboard doors were Martin. I shouted and screamed the words at him, and it felt fantastic. I cried. I laughed. I wrote and shouted and screamed until I had nothing left to say.

And then an interesting thing happened. An aliveness began flowing through my chest, my arms and legs. Colour returned to my cheeks. Life force flowed easily through my whole body. I hadn't realised how deadened I had become.

I made myself a cup of coffee and returned to write the next letter. I was keen to continue.

The other two letters were easier to write, and just as freeing and powerful. I knew it was only pretend, but the third letter touched me so deeply. I sobbed and sobbed as I wrote everything I wanted Martin to say to me, and it didn't matter that he probably never would.

While I was on a roll writing letters, I wrote two more: one to Miriam and one to Emily letting them know that by their actions I felt betrayed and that I needed some space from our friendship. I finished each letter by saying, "I hope at some point we can come together again in the love and the caring we have always shared." I sent them off in an email.

That night I slept soundly, and when the morning light peeked through the windows, I opened my eyes and stretched. My whole body felt relaxed and alive. I felt like going for a walk, but then I remembered that going for walks made the pain in my back worse. I stretched into my back to check in on it. No pain. I moved it one way and then the other way. No pain!

The pain in my back was completely gone.

I was so excited, I jumped up out of bed, still being careful with my arms, which were still sore, and went out for my walk.

Five days passed and on the sixth day Miriam responded. She apologised and asked if we could meet. She was flying back to New Zealand in two days for some work. I agreed to see her.

She held my hands and said, "Your letter made me reflect a lot, and if I never saw Martin again it wouldn't bother me, but if I didn't see you again, I would care deeply. I was trying to support both of you but I realise now that I haven't done that well. Tell me everything that happened."

We cried all afternoon and I forgave her, and apologised for not coming to her sooner.

Two more sleeps before I leave on my journey! The fighting was over. The papers were signed. The furniture stored away. The bags were packed.

I was ready.

PART 2

Open Me to trust

"It's time to fly."

Chapter 10

Looking down at my comfortable grey sneakers, I wriggled my toes. My small knapsack was slung over my shoulder, and my medium-sized grey suitcase stood by my side. These would be my traveling companions for the next two months.

The taxi was arriving at any moment.

My hand reached into the front pocket of my bag, and my fingers touched the rough surface of my passport cover, then moved to the soft plastic folder holding my ticket. A last minute check.

Even though my bags were heavy, I felt light and free. For the next two months, there was nothing I had to do apart from arriving at airports on time, attending the events I had registered for and listening to my intuition.

A friend, who was a psychic and channelled an entity called Tabaash, did a reading for me before I left, which was all good news about the trip. He said to look out for a woman called Lisa. "She's going to be a good contact for you. She'll know places and connections that will be helpful." He also said to pay attention when something got mentioned three times.

The airport was busy, and I wondered if anyone else was going on a journey like mine. But as I headed towards the check-in counter, the crowds thinned. *That's strange.* This was an international flight, and I was expecting a long queue.

When I arrived at the check-in area, there was no one there. No passengers and no airline staff. The whole area was deserted.

Did I miss the flight? I began to feel panic. I took out my ticket, but I was so distressed I couldn't read it. I waved to a passing flight attendant. "Could you please tell me the departure time for this flight?" I handed her the ticket, holding back my tears.

She smiled. "It leaves in six hours."

My panic fell away. *Six hours? How did I manage that?* I inspected my ticket again and saw that the flight attendant was right. I already had thirty hours of travel ahead of me, and I had just added six more.

I sat on a bench to assess my situation, and taking a nice, deep breath, I decided something that would greatly impact the rest of my travels: whatever happened on my journey was the journey. Whatever was happening was what was supposed to be happening, and wherever I was, that was where I was supposed to be.

I sighed, surrendering to the moment, and promptly found an airport lounge where I settled into a comfortable chair with an espresso and before I knew it I was on my flight to London via Melbourne and Hong Kong.

Waiting in the queue in Melbourne to board the next flight, I noticed a good-looking young man with blond hair and blue eyes. *His jeans fit him very well.* I blushed. I hadn't looked at a man with attraction in years. *He's probably young enough to be my son.*

While we were waiting in line, a few of us began to chat. The young man—Aaron—worked in the computer industry, and he was heading to London, too. I was having trouble with my new laptop, so I asked him about it, and he said he could look at it when we arrived in Hong Kong. I assumed he was just putting me off.

Finally we boarded and went our separate ways to our seats. I had enjoyed our little interlude.

In Hong Kong, we had a short stop to refuel and pick up more travellers, so I headed down the long corridor along with hundreds of other passengers towards the airport lounge to wait for the flight to London. At the end of the corridor, Aaron was waiting for me. My heart skipped, and we both smiled.

"Let's have a look at your laptop."

In no time Aaron had sorted out my laptop and we were boarding the next flight. "What seat are you in?" I asked him. "39E," he said. I looked at my boarding pass and my jaw dropped. *You're kidding!* We were seated next to each other.

Conversation came easily, and if I needed something, he did it for me or called the flight attendant. Even though my arms were not as inflamed as they had been, they were still very tender, and lifting my bag was difficult. I was grateful for his help and his caring. I breathed a big sigh of relief and closed my eyes as my body relaxed.

"What are you doing after your conference?" Aaron asked. "Have you ever been to Greece?" He was planning on going to Greece for a holiday after attending a friend's wedding in London.

Is he sussing out the possibility of meeting up? I imagined us swimming in the ocean, staying in a romantic villa, making love. How wonderful it would be to be held again.

I squirmed in my seat. I didn't really want to go to Greece. I did have some free time after the conference and guided tours, but I wanted to leave that time to spontaneously follow my intuition on an adventure.

I managed to change the subject. *Maybe that isn't what he is inferring anyway.* But later he brought up Greece again, and again I found myself imagining what a wonderful lover he would be. Nice and attractive as he was, though, something inside me knew that we weren't meant to be anything more to each other than seatmates on that flight.

"It's not a place that attracts me right now," I said, and immediately I felt stronger inside and I knew I had made the right choice.

In London, Aaron walked me to the bus station and showed me the bus I needed to catch. He took care of me right to the last moment. We hugged and held each other.

When we pulled apart and said good-bye, I looked up into his face, and from the very depths of my heart I said, "Thank you," as tears welled in my eyes. I was so grateful that he had been there on the first part of my journey. He had provided so much support, more than he would ever know.

"Let me know if you are thinking of Greece after your conference," he said. I nodded but I knew I wouldn't.

As one journey ended, the next one was about to begin.

Chapter 11

The sun was dipping behind the shortest buildings by the time I arrived in Glastonbury. My hand clenched the piece of paper with the address for the bed and breakfast where I was staying. The fingers of my other hand clasped the handle of my suitcase. My whole body was so weary from my travel that pulling my suitcase across the cobblestones felt as if I was dragging a trailer.

I shivered. Dusk was settling in quickly, and I didn't want to end up lost on my own so late in the day.

"Hello. Can I carry that for you?" A man in his fifties was walking beside me now. His eyes were kind. "Thank you," I said, and gladly handed him my bag, feeling grateful yet again for the support of a stranger.

I held out the piece of paper with the address and directions, and as the man read them, he shook his head. "Those directions don't make sense to me," he said. "But I know the street you are looking for. It's not far from where I live."

The man lived only a block away from where I was staying, so he walked me almost to the door, pulling my suitcase the whole way.

The bed and breakfast looked like an ordinary two-storey house, just like all the others on the street. If I hadn't had the address written down I would have walked right by. The owner lived downstairs and the guest rooms were upstairs. Two small single beds and a thin stand-up closet were squeezed into my room. Cream coloured frilly curtains framed the window and on each bed was a cream coloured doily holding a bar of soap, and two cream coloured folded towels.

The owner told me I had the double room. *How can two people fit in here?* Never having been to the United Kingdom I wondered if all rooms were this small.

I put my suitcase on the spare bed which was the only space for it. Grateful for the extra space, I unpacked my bags and crawled in between the sheets of the bed that would be mine for the next two weeks. Within minutes, I had fallen into a deep, restful sleep.

The next morning, as I walked towards the conference venue, I was feeling excited but also anxious. *There are going to be a lot of people there.* I squeezed my fingers into my palms, dreading the small talk, and conversations filled with expectations and judgments—mine!

I sighed. *Just be yourself. You are not here to impress anyone.* I exhaled as I let go of my concerns.

When I arrived at The Prophet's Conference, it was like stepping into a bustling marketplace. Hours before the five-day international event was due to begin, the big hall was already alive with hundreds of delegates, exhibitors setting up their stalls, people meeting old and new friends, and there in the middle of it all, was me.

My hand reached to my heart, feeling deep gratitude.

Walking into the main hall I thought, *I'd like to sit somewhere new for a change.* Usually I chose an aisle seat, so I can come and go as I please. This time, I broke my habit and chose a seat in the middle of a row and near the front.

As soon as the conference began, I was surprised by a tap on my shoulder. When I turned around, the woman behind me said, "Do you mind moving your shawl?" My thick, maroon woollen shawl was draped over the back of my chair, but the chairs were so tightly packed that it had fallen onto her knees. Embarrassed, I quickly folded it up and put it underneath me, hoping she didn't think I was inconsiderate.

At break time, I turned around. "Hi. I'm Leanne." The woman smiled and said, "I'm Lisa."

Lisa? Is this the *Lisa, the one Tabaash told me about?* I could hear his words in my mind, "She'll know places and connections that will be helpful."

"Would you like to chat over a coffee?" I asked.

Lisa and I promptly became friends, and ended up spending time at the conference together. We had both recently gone through separations, and it was a relief to share with someone who was going through some of the same things as me.

The speakers at the conference were inspiring and engaging, and their wealth of knowledge, insight and wisdom was intoxicating. Walking back to my accommodation at the end of each day, I felt mindfully, heartfully and soulfully sated.

Spare moments in between sessions I spent walking the cobbled streets and alleyways of Glastonbury. The shop windows were filled with magic wands, potions, feathers, crystals, tarot cards, and colourful clothing.

A book store called "The Talking Tree" was filled with every personal development and esoteric book you could imagine.

I was so excited. These were my kind of shops. I felt right at home among them and I wanted to explore every one.

A dress shop just off the main street caught my eye. I twirled to see the movement of the gorgeous light blue dress I had just tried on. It was my colour and I felt like a princess with it on. The wide flared sleeves and individually stitched skirt panels hinted the style of dresses in the King Arthur movies, and the gauzed cotton material was visibly stitched with purple threading for that unfinished chic look. It was mine!

One morning, as I was sharing breakfast with a couple of other lodgers, one of them asked, "Have you visited the Goddess Temple, Leanne?"

"No," I said, "What is it?"

The temple, she said, was a place for women to meditate, to read, to offer healings, to share. I was intrigued, and I made a mental note to go there if I happen to pass it in my wanderings.

Later that day, meandering through the exhibitors' area, I overheard snippets of a conversation between some women. Their words blended with the buzz of sound in the hall, and I wasn't actually listening but when one of them said "Goddess Temple," it caught my attention, and again I reminded myself to go there if the opportunity arose.

The next morning, I bumped into Lisa. "Good

morning!" she said. "Have you been to the Goddess Temple yet?" *Okay, I am clearly meant to go there.* Not only was this the third time I heard about it—as my psychic friend had said, "Pay attention to things that get mentioned three times"—but this time it also came from Lisa.

Right after that morning's session, I set out to find the temple. I had an inkling it was down one of the little back lanes leading off of the main street, each of which opened up to a treasure chest of more boutique shops and cafés.

I chose one of those alleyways, and followed it to an open courtyard. My eyes took in a long queue of people leading up a set of stairs towards a doorway labelled "Goddess Temple." *I found it.*

"What's happening up there," I asked someone in the queue.

"There's a shaman up there and he is offering healings for free."

A man in the Goddess Temple? This must be a special occasion and he must be very good.

My attention moved to my arms which were still a bit tender. This was the perfect place to be, and the timing could not have been better.

As my place in the queue got closer to the stairs I noticed people leaving the front of the line coming back down the stairs and walking away. "Excuse me," I said to one of them. "Is the shaman finished?"

"He's fully booked," she said. "The temple is packed. There's no way anyone else is going to get to see him."

I frowned. *Darn. What an incredible opportunity, and now I am going to miss it*. More people left the queue. *I could get some lunch. I am hungry*. I remained standing in the queue. It didn't feel right to leave.

Why am I still waiting in line? What if I spend all this time just to be told what people are already telling me? Then I realised there was no reason to be anxious about wasting time. I had nowhere to be. *Where do I feel like being right now?* The answer I got was that it felt right to be exactly where I was, in the queue. So I stayed, and the anxiety left.

The woman at the temple doorway was dressed in a flowing pink goddess gown which fit her voluptuous figure perfectly. Her dark brown, thick hair hung loosely around her shoulders and she held a commanding air about her. She was beautiful. I looked down at my simple summer top and shorts, feeling a little frumpy. "I'm sorry the temple is full," I heard her say to the people in front of me. They turned around and headed back down the stairs.

It really didn't matter to me that she was going to turn me away too. I was actually enjoying simply waiting in line, doing nothing.

The goddess looked at me next. "I'm sorry, the shaman is fully booked," she said.

I smiled and said, "That's okay. I just want to be in this lovely space."

It didn't matter that I wouldn't have a healing with the shaman.

There was no one left in the line in front of me. They

had all given up and gone away. I poked my head inside the temple door. Inside was one large room, and it was packed. Some people were lucky to have chairs; others were sitting on the floor or standing.

Just as I was contemplating walking away, the goddess touched my shoulder and pointed to a corner of the room where eight colourfully-dressed, human-sized mannequins were arranged in a circle. "That is the Goddess circle," she said to me. "You can sit inside there. I will ask the shaman if he can fit you in when he has finished, but I can't promise anything."

My eyes lit up, and my heart spilled over with appreciation. "Thank you," I said, and as I made my way inside, I heard her turn away the people behind me.

Negotiating my way around and over the sea of bodies, I reached the Goddess circle. A mat had been placed on the floor in the middle. At least four people could have fit inside the circle, but I had the whole space to myself.

I looked around the room. Everyone here was waiting for a healing. It would take hours. I looked at the clock, which said it was just after one in the afternoon. My stomach growled, and for a fleeting second I contemplated staying briefly and then leaving. But having come this far, having followed what felt right, having been offered a space in that room, I was committed to staying there, no matter what. *What do I care how long it takes? I am here to hang out in this healing energy until the right moment comes for me to leave.*

I lay down on the mat and closed my eyes. Slowly,

I began to surrender my mind to the sounds of people breathing. Then I heard the loud breathing of the shaman and a wooshing sound, followed by wailing. My eyes opened again. *What is going on? What is he doing? What is that wailing? Is he making those sounds or does he have some kind of instrument?*

I sat up to check if I could see anything, but I couldn't. A thick curtain covered the end of the room where the shaman was working. I looked around the room, but no one else appeared disturbed. They were all just waiting their turn.

I lay back down, and the next thing I knew, I was startled by a gentle whispering in my ear. "The shaman will see you now," the goddess said, smiling. I nodded and sat up. The temple was empty. The clock said it was just after five. *How has the time passed by without my noticing? I must have fallen asleep or something.*

But I didn't feel like I had been sleeping. I felt like I had been meditating. Looking down at the floor I thought, *I lay unmoving on my back on the hardwood floor for almost four hours. That was some meditation.*

"You will find him behind that curtain," she said, and then she walked away. I hadn't expected to have a healing, and I had never met or even seen a shaman before, so I was curious and excited.

Behind the curtain, I found a big man in his early forties with red hair and glasses. He was wearing a plain white T-shirt and sitting in a plastic chair next to a massage table. I didn't know what I was expecting, but I was surprised to find that he looked like an ordinary guy—no feathers or special head gear.

"What brought you here?" he asked.

I sighed. *Where do I start? Should I tell him the whole story?* I decided to keep it short. Taking a deep breath, I said the words that were there to say. "Deep grief." Those two words covered everything I had been through. I didn't even think to tell him about my arms, and he didn't ask any more questions.

He indicated for me to lie down on the massage table, and he explained that he would stand about a metre away from my body to do his work. He made some opening prayers, calling in the divine help he needed, and began his work immediately. I closed my eyes and called in all of my divine help.

Soon the wooshing sound began. *Hah! There it is!* For a brief second I almost opened my eyes to find out what was making that sound, but I didn't. I knew if I opened my eyes, my mind would begin to judge what he was doing and try to figure things out. I wanted to experience the healing and not be in my head about it. I kept my eyes shut. It didn't matter if I knew.

Then he began to wail. It was that same deep, grieving sound I had heard before, but even deeper. Such powerful tones came from his voice that they vibrated through my body. Tremors, like waves, moved through me, and at times I wanted to sob, the feelings were so strong. Then they subsided, and I felt relief.

I didn't know what he was doing, but my body became completely still. I was almost unable to move.

After a while, he said, "Okay. We're done." I sat up

slowly and glanced at the clock. It was almost six. "How do you feel?" he asked. Everything looked new and fresh, as if my eyes were seeing things for the first time. The healing had been very powerful.

"I feel emotionally raw and opened, but in a good way."

"I wasn't going to do any more healings," he said. "I've been going non-stop since this morning and I was feeling wiped out. But I am very grateful I did this one. I have never done a session like that before."

"What do you mean?"

"The energies that worked through me were so powerful they completely took over my body," he said, smiling. "I feel wholly replenished."

My feet didn't touch the ground as I walked back to the bed and breakfast. I went straight to my room, and slept soundly.

In the morning, when I woke, my arms were completely healed.

Chapter 12

Should I wear a skirt or pants? I stood in front of the mirror holding up each option for consideration. The conference was now over and fifty of the delegates had registered for the guided tours to sacred sites in and around Glastonbury. Today was our first visit.

I figured if I wore the skirt I would have to be adjusting it all the time getting in and out of the bus, and I'd also have to wear the right shoes which might not be the best for walking. I decided on the loose black pants and my grey sneakers. I looked down at my sneakers. *They don't go very well with the black pants. Comfort or style?* I kept them on.

I was disappointed that Lisa couldn't make it. She had to go back to work. We had got on so well, and she encouraged me to go to the Goddess Temple and had confirmed my choice of The Shadow Process—it was one of her favourite courses. I knew we would stay in touch.

Sitting on the bus on the way to Stonehenge, I turned to Donna, the woman sitting beside me, and said, "I am so excited."

"Me too!" She grabbed my arm. We both laughed.

I spotted another woman on the bus who was looking very fashionable. I leaned over to check out her outfit. Black well-tailored pants, black lace up shoes and a small black funky knapsack. I looked down at my grey sneakers and my baggy black pants. I wanted her shoes and her bag. Actually I wanted her hair. It was long, thick and straight—very different from my wispy blonde locks.

My attention moved to my sneakers again and I wriggled my toes. *If we do a lot of walking I'm going to be glad I'm wearing these.* I fluffed my hair and looked out the window, deciding to be happy to be in my shoes and not hers.

Unlike my feet, my tummy wasn't very happy at all. It was sore, and I wondered if it was all the excitement and my nerves, although it didn't usually feel this bad. *Maybe it was something I ate.* I put my hand on my belly. *This isn't a good time to feel sick. I don't want to miss any of this.*

I tried to ignore the pain, but the closer we got to our destination, the stronger it became.

At sunset, the bus pulled into a deserted parking lot. Our group had special permission to be at Stonehenge in the evening, which made it even more mysterious and exciting. Scanning the area, I spotted the stones. I had seen pictures, but nothing could have prepared me for seeing them in person.

Huge, roughly rectangular shaped stones, eight to nine metres tall, had been placed in a large circle in a field, thousands of years ago. It is believed that some of the stones came from thirty-two kilometres away. The people who constructed the site left no records or clues as to the purpose of this structure.

Ignoring my aching stomach, I pulled my shawl around me as we walked in silence towards the stones. My heart was pounding as if something important was about to happen.

The pain in my belly seemed to get worse the closer I got. *The timing of this is terrible.* I kept walking determined to not let the pain stop me. Standing still for a moment I closed my eyes, breathing deeply into the ache. It eased a bit.

Our tour guide beckoned us to enter the stone circle. I stepped in slowly and consciously. As soon as both feet landed inside the circle, I heard voices say, "Welcome home." The stones were speaking to me, and I could hear them.

Why are they welcoming me home? Have I been here before?

Wandering around the circle of huge stone columns, I tried to imagine what it might have been used for. A growing number of speculations existed about its purpose. Some theories said it was used as a burial ground, or for celebrations and rituals; others indicated it might have been used for healing purposes, or for music, or that it had something to do with the sun. But no one really knew.

The red sun was low in the sky as it shone through the stone structure. Our guide said the stones might have messages for us and to pay attention to where we felt inclined to go. One of the large ones in the archway attracted me. I ran my hand down its side, feeling the rough surface as I sat down and leaned my back into it closing my eyes. As soon as I was still, it spoke to me, saying, "It's time to fly, Leanne."

Sitting there I reflected for a moment. The message had come quickly and easily, and it had gone to the depths of my consciousness. At some level I understood it completely, but at another level I was confused. *What does that mean? How am I supposed to fly?*

As I held these questions in my mind, an image came to me of a butterfly emerging from its chrysalis. The stone spoke again. "How does a butterfly learn to fly?" I watched the vision in my mind as the butterfly opened up its wings for the first time while still holding on to its cocoon. Moving its wings as if to get a feel for them, it finally let go, and flew. I opened my eyes and kept my attention on the ground in front of me, digesting the message. In my periphery I noticed movements of the other travellers around me.

My attention was drawn by our tour guide speaking. I touched the stone and whispered, "Thank you," as I got up to move closer to the group. The guide said the energy was the strongest in the centre of the circle. I felt an intense pull to go there. Up to that point, I was only just managing the pain in my belly through breathing and conscious movement. Now, with each step I took towards the centre, the pain amplified.

I kept moving. Finally I stood with my feet in the centre of the circle. I closed my eyes to feel the energy, but the pain was excruciating. I breathed deeply into my hand on my belly, but there was no relief. My head felt light and dizzy. A fuzzy feeling coated my lips, and my mouth watered with the sour taste of nausea.

Finally I couldn't take the pain anymore. I knew I had to move away. Afraid of losing consciousness, I staggered out of the circle and distanced myself from the stones. I fell to my knees on some grass and leaned forward with my forehead touching the cool earth. It was soothing.

Within seconds, I was sobbing, deep, loud, uncontrollable sobs into the earth. I didn't feel upset, and I wasn't sure what I was crying about, but whatever it was, it needed to come out.

I had never cried like that before, and by the time the sobs subsided I felt emptied, clear and at peace. The pain in my stomach had gone. My forehead was still on the ground when I felt a big bug fly into my head and get tangled in my hair. Yanking my head up, I frantically batted at my hair to untangle the poor beetle.

I laughed. *How quickly things change.* I thought about how funny it must have all looked.

The sky was getting dark, and it was time to go back. Donna had stayed nearby me, to make sure I was okay. We walked arm in arm back to the bus. I couldn't explain to her what the pain had been about and what had just happened, but I felt wonderful. I was lighter and clearer, and all the pain had gone.

Chapter 13

The following day on our next tour, I stepped out of the bus and looked up toward a blue sky scattered with a few clouds. There was a slight nippiness in the breeze as I turned to look down West Kennet Avenue, a pre-historic site in Avebury, dating four thousand, six hundred years old[2]. This avenue had been created by two rows of tall standing stones, averaging three metres in height—one hundred on each side in its original state—creating a two-and-a-half-kilometre corridor leading to a large standing stone circle.

Donna and another woman were chatting a few metres away, and I felt like joining them. *I wonder if I'll be interrupting them.* I shook my hair, shaking away the self-doubt, and went over.

"Yes!" the other woman said when she saw me. "We were looking for a third person, and it's you. Hi, I'm Angellica." She reached out to take my hand.

It felt good to be wanted, but I had no idea what she was talking about. "What do you mean?" I said.

"Donna and I were saying that it feels like we are meant to do some energy work here, and we knew we needed a third person," she said. "You're the one."

I didn't know what she meant by "energy work," but

---

[2] According to the National Trust, Charitable Organisation, Swindon, England

it felt right to be there with them, so I decided to be open and trust.

Along with fifty fellow travellers, the three of us began the two-and-a-half kilometre walk along the avenue. As we walked we shared about our lives. Angellica had separated from her husband, but they were still living in the family home together. She had recently met someone new, and it was becoming increasingly uncomfortable at home.

I shuddered, recalling my own experience with Martin. "How can you do that and still take care of yourself?" I asked her. She said it was hard but that she was afraid of supporting herself financially on her own.

I understood that one too.

Donna had two small children and had always wanted to travel. She had finally organised for her children's father, from whom she was divorced, to take care of them so she could fulfil her dream of visiting these sacred sites.

As we continued our walk, I began to have flashbacks to another period a very long time ago. In my vision, hundreds of people, our skin varying shades of light and dark olive tones, all dressed in simple white robes, were walking together along the avenue towards the large stone circle, just like we were doing now. With each step, I felt the echoes of lifetimes walking with me, heading towards something important, maybe a special meeting or ceremony.

The dry grass crunched beneath my sandals. *Was the ground like this when they walked it?*

When we neared the end of the avenue, just before reaching the stone circle, I snuggled into one of the big stones, out of the breeze, and looked for Donna and Angellica. To my surprise, they had turned around to face the direction we had just come from and were standing side by side with their eyes closed and their arms outstretched.

The rest of our tour-mates were milling around, waiting for our guide to catch up with us. I felt an inclination to go and join my two friends, but what they were doing looked weird, and I didn't want to look weird. Then I remembered Angellica saying, "We are meant to do some energy work here..." *Is this the moment? What if it turns out to be nothing and we end up standing there looking silly?*

The tension inside me grew. I was either going to keep hanging onto the rock, just like I was clinging to my thoughts, doubts and fears, or I was going to let it all go and act.

I moved in beside Angellica and Donna. Placing my body the same distance they were from each other, I closed my eyes and held my arms out in exactly the same position as theirs.

And then something truly astonishing happened.

The very moment I placed my body and limbs at the same angles as theirs and closed my eyes, I heard something, or rather felt something click into place, as if the three of us now formed a perfect pattern with our bodies.

In my mind, I saw an arch of white light form above

us in a grid pattern. Beams of light from this grid began to shoot out and down through the avenue. We held our positions with our eyes closed for nearly ten minutes while this light continued to flow from the arched grid above our heads and down between the standing stones.

Neither Donna, Angellica, nor I spoke or looked at each other to discuss any of this. Each, in our own way, was trusting and following some intuitive guidance.

What exactly is happening here?

The answer came clearly and quickly, quicker than my own thoughts. I understood that we were re-opening an old runway of light that had been used long, long ago, which would now be needed once again.

I had no idea what this message meant, and I didn't feel a need to understand. Whatever we were doing and whatever was happening felt satisfying and uplifting. I trusted that and knew it was good.

The conversation with Donna and Angellica that evening over dinner was extraordinary. No one knew who had instigated our energy work. Donna said it wasn't her, and so did Angellica. It certainly wasn't me. As we talked, we discovered that we'd each felt the same powerful light flowing through us down between the stones, and we had all known the exact moment to stop. When I shared with them the message I had received, the excitement in our voices became even greater.

It was almost two in the morning when I walked up the stairs to my room, and a big ball of orange tabby fur was waiting for me at my bedroom door. It was Sammy, the house cat. We headed straight to bed, and my last blurry thought before falling asleep was, *What new experiences will tomorrow bring?*

Chapter 14

I pulled my pink top over my head. *A perfect colour for this feminine energy day.*

Our guide said that the site we were going to visit was known for its strong, feminine energy. I was curious to know how 'feminine energy' was defined and wondered how it would express itself in a geographical location.

I reached for my grey sneakers. *Not very feminine but my feet love them.* Stepping outside I set out for the ten minute walk to the tour bus. The sun was hazy through the clouds, leaving its warmth behind and creating a cool mist. I pulled my wool shawl closer around my neck. The fog created an atmosphere of mystery and anticipation for what lay ahead.

Cerne Abbas was the quaint little village where the bus dropped us off. Actually, all of the villages and the small towns we visited were quaint, characterised by their brick and stone buildings and the abundant colourful flowers spilling out of pots perched on the many windowsills.

Our guide led us to a dirt path hugged by tall overhanging trees that created the impression we were entering a deep forest. Our chatter subsided. Even Donna, Angellica and I, who had become inseparable since our experience at Avebury, walked side by side in silence. The only sound was the gentle padding of our feet.

My mind was quiet. Rich smells of composting earth rose from the ground, and I breathed them in deeply. The dappled light played through the thick canopy of trees, bringing a feeling of magic to the air.

St. Augustine's Well, also known as Silver Well, was at the end of the path. Surrounded by bush and trees, it felt private and intimate. Our guide told us that for centuries the water had been believed to have special healing powers. Although, today, some still may find it healing, the well has come to be regarded more as a peaceful place to meditate and relax. The villagers still used the water from the well for drinking to this day.

I felt a strong inclination to put my feet in the water, but I hesitated. *What if people think I'm being disrespectful? Surely I shouldn't put my feet in the water if people still drink it.* I paused. Others in the group were standing looking at the water. One person knelt down to touch it. Another filled up their water bottle, and someone else put some crystals in it. "Trust," I whispered to myself as I untied my shoe laces.

I sat down on the smooth, rock edge, like the edge of a swimming pool. The water was about thirty centimetres deep. Slipping my feet in, I closed my eyes so that I could completely focus on the sensation of the water on my feet. A soothing coolness flowed up into the centre of my chest, and I felt an opening in my lungs as if I had inhaled eucalyptus.

After a few minutes, I pulled my feet out. Someone else put their feet in. People were still milling around the well and touching the water but no one was speaking. My mind was in a state of reverie, as if I was in a waking dream. From time to time I heard the gentle murmur of the tour guide's voice as he pointed out one thing or another.

As I looked into the well, a delightful melody reached my ears. *Am I dreaming? Or am I really hearing this?* I listened more intently. It was a real voice of a woman softly humming. Focusing on the sound of her voice, I lost awareness of the fifty other people close by.

I wanted to join with the sound and hum too. *I haven't sung in a long time. I might be off key.* But I put my thoughts aside, and a hum began to flow from my throat. My voice joined the other woman's voice. We weren't humming any song that I knew, but our voices began to naturally dance together. At first our humming was very soft, barely audible, but as our confidence grew, our voices became stronger. The sound was delightful, luscious, and sensual.

I closed my eyes, and immediately a vision appeared from a time long ago.

> *A group of women gathered at this well to bathe. Each woman kept to herself, and each hummed her own tune, and yet all of their tunes danced together instinctively. None of them directly interacted, and yet their unspoken togetherness created a powerful intimacy that was supportive and nurturing.*

Our humming eventually subsided and stopped. Silence. Stillness. Peace. My awareness slowly drifted back to my present reality, and I became conscious again of the other travellers. I opened my eyes and looked around to see who I had been humming with. A gorgeous, glowing face was smiling at me. It was Angellica. We laughed and hugged.

As we headed back up the path towards the bus, Angellica and I walked hand in hand. "I had this incredible vision," I said to her. I started to share with her what I had seen, but she interrupted me part way through.

"We were all humming, weren't we?" she said.

I turned to look at her, amazed. "Yes," I said.

She squeezed my arm. "I saw the same thing."

My heart was over-flowing with love for life, but the magic wasn't finished.

I hadn't seen Donna in a while, and just as I turned to look for her she appeared, coming over a small hill from the other direction to join us on the path. Her cheeks and eyes were red and tear-stained. "Are you okay, Donna?" Angellica reached out to her. Donna smiled and nodded. Her eyes sparkled.

"I was sitting in a tree over there listening to the birds and meditating," she pointed to an area far away from where we had been. "Then I heard the most magnificent, heavenly voices. The angels were singing to me, and I received the most powerful healing from them."

Angellica and I looked at each other, and our eyes widened. Our humming had been too soft for Donna to have heard us from that far away, and besides, the well was completely surrounded by bush.

"That was us, Donna," Angellica and I said in unison.

We all stood there with our hearts and our mouths wide open, speechless.

After the experience at the well, I still couldn't define what feminine energy was, but I could feel it, and it was powerful. It went deep to wherever it was needed, it knew no limits, and it uplifted all.

Chapter 15

A soft meow sounded at my door. When I opened it, Sammy came in and jumped on my bed. He had taken to sleeping with me every night. Even though I loved traveling on my own, sometimes in the evenings I felt lonely, so it was comforting to have another presence with me. I looked into Sammy's eyes. They partially closed as his purring grew louder, and I knew he felt the same way.

I turned out the light and got into bed, but my mind was still wide awake, so I scratched Sammy's head and reflected on the past ten days. Day one at the conference seemed like a lifetime ago, and I felt sad that my two weeks in Glastonbury, a place where I had experienced so much magic, would soon be coming to an end.

I hadn't yet decided where I was going to spend the following two weeks. I had been waiting for something to catch my attention or for some divinely ordained meeting to guide me in the right direction, but nothing like that had happened.

Early the next morning I opened my computer. Lisa had replied to my email asking where she recommended I go. I was considering maybe Scotland or Ireland. But she didn't say either of them. Instead she said, "I think you would love Malta."

Malta? Why is she saying to go to Malta? I don't know anything about Malta.

Her email said when she went there she had had a powerful experience at a temple called Mnajdra. The hairs on my arms stood on end. She said Malta had the oldest surviving temples in the world. Some of them were thought to be up to ten thousand years old.

Now I was excited.

Questions filled my mind, but something inside told me I didn't really need to know anything more. I had already decided to go.

I bought my ticket that morning. I was going to Malta.

Later in the day, I began sharing with other people on the tour about my plans to go to Malta. Their responses were alarmingly mixed. I had expected everyone to say how fabulous it would be, but they didn't. Some said that it was an amazing place and I would love it, but most questioned my choice and told me that it was the worst time to visit—July and August being the hottest months of the year.

My excitement vanished quickly. An image of the ticket in my purse came to my mind, and I began wondering if I could get a refund. *Why is summer so bad? I love the heat.* But I wondered if people's comments were indicating that I really should go somewhere else.

Trying to lift my spirits again I imagined what it would be like in Malta. I'd never been there or even seen pictures of it, so it was easy to fantasise about an exotic and romantic place where I could relax by the water and do nothing. *What can go wrong with that? And besides, a bit more heat would be nice.* But I was still feeling uneasy.

Later that day, I went back to my room to prepare for

dinner. As I pulled out some clothes from my suitcase, I felt a presence in the room. I turned. No one was there. I continued getting ready, but I could still feel it.

Then in my peripheral vision, I saw a woman with long, black hair, olive skin and dark eyes. Her eyes weren't just dark in colour, they were dark with anger, and that anger was directed at me. I felt it.

I turned to look at her straight on, but I couldn't see her.

I'm just imagining this, I told myself as chills went through me. I had seen apparitions before, but none had ever been so menacing.

I shook my head to get her out of my thoughts and carried on getting ready.

When I came home after dinner that night, Sammy wasn't there. He didn't come into my room all night, and sleep eluded me for hours as I tossed and turned.

Over the next couple of days, the angry woman spirit returned two more times, making it a total of three visits. I tried to ignore her, but the vision persisted. I tried asking her what she wanted, but she wouldn't respond. She just stared at me with her angry eyes. Each time, she stayed for about five minutes and then vanished.

One evening, I was lying in bed writing my reflections for the day. Sammy was curled up by my feet. As my pen glided on the page, it occurred to me that the apparition of the angry woman came to me three times. That meant I needed to pay attention to her. Then, all of a sudden it dawned on me. She started appearing right after I bought my ticket for Malta. *She has something to do with my going there!*

Tingles ran down my spine. *Maybe going there really isn't such a good idea.*

I put my pen down. *What should I do? People are saying it's a bad time to go. Are these warning signs?* A feeling of trepidation rose in my chest. *It's not too late to change my ticket and go somewhere else.* I considered my options.

Part of the issue, I realised, was that I didn't want to leave Glastonbury. I wanted to keep getting up every morning, meeting my friends at the bus and going on remarkable adventures to sacred sites. I wanted to come back home to the bed and breakfast, crawl into my familiar bed with Sammy at my feet and sleep soundly. I didn't want to leave my comfortable new routine and go and face new challenges in an unknown place. I had just come from a broken marriage with all the challenges I could handle.

I reminded myself that I hadn't come to Europe on a holiday. The purpose of my journey was to let go of my fears and follow my intuition—going to Malta would allow me to do both. *If I change my ticket now, I'll feel like I missed out on something important. I have to go.*

I gulped. I knew something was coming that was going to test me, but whatever it was, I was determined to hold on to the trust that it was meant to happen. With my decision made, I turned back to my journaling, a new state of alertness flowing through my veins.

Chapter 16

"Here's to friendship," Donna said as she raised her glass of wine. The lump in my throat made it difficult for me to smile as I raised mine. She, Angellica and I were sharing our last meal together. In the morning, I was leaving for Malta, Angellica was heading back home to deal with her situation—feeling more confidence now—and Donna had managed to extend her travels to visit more sacred sites.

I was going to miss them. I had felt so normal with them. To them it was normal to see spirits and other entities, to hear voices and to do 'weird' things like energy healing. We had shared so much in such a short time.

As we parted, we hugged and cried, promising to meet again in some other sacred place someday.

My magical time in Glastonbury had come to an end.

As I crawled into my little bed for the last time, it occurred to me that I hadn't seen the angry woman apparition in the last two days. I had already forgotten about her. I smiled and closed my eyes.

When I woke up, it was still dark. I pressed the button on my clock to illuminate the digital numbers. Four fifty eight. My alarm was about to go off and a taxi would be there to pick me up in half an hour. I'd had a restless night with disturbing dreams that I couldn't remember.

I pictured the luxurious bed and breakfast I had booked in Malta. It looked like an exotic palace in the photos on the website. *It doesn't matter how tired I am. I can spend the next several days lounging by the water.*

I reached for Sammy to say goodbye, but he was gone. The warmth of the bedcovers told me he had just left. Tears began to well in my eyes. Closing them I brought him to my mind and imagined myself thanking him for his comfort and companionship. I felt my love for him flow out of my heart to wherever he was.

The sun had only just risen, and everyone else in the house was still sleeping, so I was careful to shut the gate quietly behind me. I affectionately caressed the top of the gate and whispered, "Thank you."

The plane landed in Malta with a jolt. I woke up, startled, and gripped the arm rests. *Have I slept the whole three hours of flight?* I felt groggy and tired. I tried to take a deep breath to wake myself up, but I couldn't. My nose was swollen and sore. In Glastonbury, I had caught a cold, but it was almost gone. I wondered if something in the air on the plane had made it worse.

Well at least I was looking forward to stepping out of the plane and getting a blast of summer warmth. I loved that deep, warm bone-soothing feeling. The summer in Glastonbury was cool. But when I took my first step out of the plane, I gasped. The intensity of the heat was so suffocating that I couldn't breathe at all. It was like walking into a hot oven.

My clothes clung to me like cling-wrap. I pulled the neck of my dress away from my skin to let some air flow, but the hot air rushed down my top, burning my neck. Quickly, my fingers released the material, leaving it to stick to me again. I wasn't sure which felt worse.

I held the railing tightly to steady myself as I descended onto the tarmac. *I'm probably just tired and in need of a good rest.* I was looking forward to settling in at the bed and breakfast and relaxing by the pool. *There will be a pool, won't there?* I gripped the railing tighter. I didn't recall a pool being mentioned on the website, but I told myself that surely in such a hot country every tourist accommodation had to have one.

As soon as I set foot on the runway, I ran into the airport building, knowing it would be air conditioned, and stood just inside the doors sucking in the cool, processed air with relief. Finally I could breathe.

"Would you like a GPS?" the man at the rental car desk asked as he handed me the keys to a small, white car. I had never used a GPS, and I didn't like using gadgets. Besides, it cost fifty dollars a day to rent one, and over ten days that would be a big saving.

"No thank you," I said confidently, patting the map I had just received from the information centre. The woman there had highlighted the entire route I needed to take to get to where I was staying. *I have all the help I need.* The map was clear and simple. Not to mention the fact that the whole of Malta was so small I could drive from one end to the other in two hours. *How can I possibly get lost?*

Before I drove out of the rental car parking lot, I sat in the stifling hot car for a moment and closed my eyes.

Here I was, finally in Malta. *Okay so it's a bit hotter than I imagined, but this is my journey.* My nose was stuffy, my eyes were now inflamed, and my cold was definitely back. All I wanted to do was to curl up and go to bed. *At least I can go straight to my accommodation and have a nice cold shower.*

The woman at the information centre said it wasn't more than an hour away, meaning I should get there before noon. With my map splayed out on the seat beside me, I was ready to go.

I pulled out of the airport and looked for the street sign I needed, but I couldn't see it. The road was separating into three. The map showed only one road. Needing to make a decision quickly, I picked the road on the right. That took me to a round-about which offered another three options, none of which were on my map. I drove around the round-about several times reading each road sign just to make sure.

A couple of car horns honked at me, and I could feel the heat of embarrassment rise into my neck. My shoulders raised as I thought, *I'm sorry. I'm a tourist and I don't know where I am going.*

After numerous failed attempts to find my way, I started to panic, so I pulled over. An hour had already gone by, and I had no idea where I was.

I looked up in the sky at the sun directly overhead. *I don't even know which direction I am facing.*

Trying to keep myself focused, I scrutinised my map and the answer became obvious. The map was too simplified to be a helpful street map, and it was in English, while all the street signs were in Maltese, a language that bore no resemblance to English whatsoever.

I saw the map for what it was: a colourful cartoon of Malta, something to hang on the wall as a souvenir. *How could that woman have given this to me? Did she not realise it couldn't be followed?* I pushed the useless map onto the floor and rummaged through the glove compartment for another map. Nothing.

Leaning back in my seat, I rubbed my sore eyes. I tried to relax and breathe deeply, but I was already fighting back tears. My right hand patted the steering wheel as my chin began to quiver. I bit my lip, trying to keep it still. *I'm not lost. I can't be lost.* I needed to reassure myself. Being lost was up there among my top fears.

I knew I needed to pull myself together, but all I really wanted was someone to come along and show me the way. *This is too hard.* I shook my head, and tears stung my eyes.

All the divine guidance I had thought was with me had vanished. I was on my own.

The angry spirit woman came to my mind. I hadn't thought of her at all until then. *Does she have anything to do with this?* I wondered suspiciously. *Did I make the wrong choice? Maybe those people were right. Maybe I should have gone to Scotland. Maybe I should have gone to Greece. Maybe I shouldn't have to come Malta.* My panic was rising.

Maybe this really was the wrong choice.

Chapter 17

"Come on Leanne. You have to deal with this," I said out loud. I focused my attention. "Okay, I am in this car, in a country where I have never been. I don't know where north is. I have a map I can't read. But I know where I'm going because I have the address."

I decided to ask the locals for help.

Each person I asked was very friendly and clearly wanted to help, but their lack of English, my lack of Maltese, the fact they couldn't understand my map either (which in a perverse way made me feel better) meant that I could only travel about one kilometre at a time before I needed to stop and ask for help again.

Slowly, I inched my way.

The sun was low in the sky when I finally stood at the ornate wrought iron entrance to the bed and breakfast. Reaching out my weary hand to open the gate, I couldn't be bothered to be curious about my surroundings. My clothes were damp, my skin was sticky, my eyes were red and stinging, my nose was sore and runny, and I was shattered.

An attractive, tall and slender young woman with straight, shoulder length brown hair opened the door, "You must be Leanne. You look like a goddess!" she said with a big, welcoming smile. I felt very ungodess-like, but her comment perked me up a bit.

"We thought you weren't coming," she said, helping me with my suitcase. *I thought I wasn't coming too.* But I didn't tell her about my travels. I was too tired to talk.

"Do you have a swimming pool?" I asked.

"No, but we have a hot tub," she said. *A hot tub? Why would anyone want to be in a hot tub here?*

My room was a smaller version of the rest of the house, full of carved, handmade wooden furniture, rich textiles, elaborate rugs, intriguing wall hangings, and large tropical plants. It really was like a palace.

It was hot in the room, even in the evening, and I looked around for the air conditioning unit, but there wasn't one. In the corner stood a small portable fan. *Is that it? How do people live in this heat without air conditioning?*

I showered and got straight into the bed. Even the thin cotton sheets felt like heavy blankets. The fan blew hot air at me, and I lay awake watching the last of the sun melting below the horizon. The gentle cool of the night finally replaced the heat of the day, and my heavy eyelids surrendered into that delicious peaceful state just on the edge of sleep.

"Zzzzzzzzz..." The familiar and dreaded sound of a mosquito buzzing near my head. My eyes blinked open. *How can mosquitos live here? Everything is so dry.* What was even more intriguing was that it was able to fly even with the fan blowing at full speed. Pulling the sheet up over my head, I decided that I would leave in the morning. Practical concerns, such as how I was going to find a travel agent and choose a more restful holiday destination, ran through my mind as I fell into an agitated sleep.

Long forgotten in the recesses of my mind was the knowing that I had been guided here.

I spent the following two days deliriously sick in bed, unable to go out, managing only to get up for a meal each day kindly prepared for me by the young woman's mother. On day three, feeling weak but a little better, I pushed myself up to venture out for a walk.

Everything outside was white. All the dwellings were attached, so from the top of the street it seemed as if there was only one very large and long building made of white plaster. Even the street was white cement. It was another starkly bright and sunny day, and the intense light of the sun on the expanse of whiteness hurt my eyes. I held my hands up as a shield. My skin was burning from the strong sun, and I was struggling to breathe. My body was still so tender and tired from the flu I was still getting over. I felt miserable and disappointed.

The landscape of Malta gave me no pleasure, either. Apart from the occasional tree, the land was sunburnt and barren. The only green plants I saw were in pots. There was nothing lush or exotic about Malta at all.

I had lost all trust that I had made the right choice by coming there. The powerful, peaceful state I had experienced for most of my trip was gone.

As I walked along the street looking down at my feet I heard Lisa's voice in my mind, "You would love Malta." I knew she had written that in an email but I could hear her voice saying it. *I'm not really loving Malta*

125

now. Then I remembered reading her email and feeling chills go through my body. I had felt so certain about coming here.

In that instant something shifted inside and I decided I had had enough of being miserable.

Speaking out loud to the block of white houses, I said, "If I've come to Malta for a reason, then let's get this show on the road!"

In the town centre, I found a tour bus going to a few temples, and on the list of stops I recognised the name Mnajdra. I knew that was where I needed to start. I could have taken my little white rental car, but even thinking about driving made me tremble. Having someone else drive would be much more relaxing.

Mnajdra was the last site we visited on the tour that day. As the bus pulled into the gate, I could feel my heart beating. I eagerly looked around for the temple, but dry bush and dead grass was all I could see. I went straight to the information kiosk. "Excuse me," I said. "Where can I find the temple Mnajdra?"

The old man behind the counter gave me a map of the area. He started to tell me about another temple I could visit at the site, but I wasn't interested. "I want to go straight to Mnajdra."

He paused and pulled down his glasses to look at me. Then he asked me a strange question. "Why do you want to go to Mnajdra?" His eyes looked deep into mine, and we stayed looking at each other in silence for a few seconds. In his eyes I saw a knowing, a knowing that I was there for a deeper reason and not just a tourist visit.

Finally I spoke. From deep within my heart I said, "I'm not sure. I have a feeling I have to go there."

"I thought so," he said. Then he smiled. Our eyes connected for a few more seconds as if our souls were remembering something beyond words.

The map indicated it was almost a kilometre walk to the temple. When I stepped out of the information kiosk and back into the intense heat, dry bush and burnt grass was still all I could see.

I walked slowly along the path toward Mnajdra, feeling my feet take each step. I wanted to fully experience being here, paying attention to all of my senses.

I was in no hurry.

Chapter 18

As I walked the thin, worn dirt trail, my eyes scanned the horizon: clear blue sky, the dry land in front of me jutting out to a point, and beyond it the deep blue of the ocean. I could see the temple in the distance.

My arms swayed by my side. My feet felt the ground beneath them. My eyes fixed on the temple surrounded by blue. Something about this felt so familiar, as if I had done it many times before. Goose bumps raised on my arms.

For a moment, my mind got caught up with questions. *How can this feel familiar? I haven't been here before. Am I making this up?* But my doubts quickly disappeared as I brought my attention back to the present moment and the feelings in my body.

Other tourists were coming and going, but I didn't pay any attention to them.

The white stone, Neolithic temple was among the oldest still-standing temples in the world. In its original state, estimated five and a half thousand years ago, it was suspected to have had a roof. The remaining stones sculpted clearly the shape of the temple complex consisting of three rooms, covering nearly three thousand square metres[3].

---

[3] According to UNESCO World Heritage Site, the temple complex covered a land area of 2,890 m²

The temple was built near the edge of the cliff at the end of the headland, with ocean views on three sides. My whole being was taken in by its beauty. The warm ocean breeze brushed my skin, and I breathed it all in— as best as I could with my nose still stuffy—feeling the contrast of the humid ocean air and the dry dusty earth.

Just before stepping into the physical space of the temple, I paused to take in the whole scene. Then, inside my head, I heard a voice say, "This is why you've come." My body became more alert. I knew I was in the right place.

Moving slowly, I paid attention to where I felt attracted to go as I began to explore. I was in my own world, even though at least a dozen other tourists were also walking around the temple. When I stepped down from what seemed to be a platform of some kind, a small voice sounded in my head. "You're not leaving already are you?" The voice took me by surprise, but it didn't frighten me. It sounded like the voice of a child and all I felt was love.

"No, I'm not leaving yet," I said telepathically. "I'm wandering around so I can see more."

A small stone wall, less than a metre high, going around one side of the temple caught my attention. Many stones, varying in sizes from the dimensions of my hand to larger, had been perfectly fit together to create this wall. It was exquisite, and I knelt down to touch it. The cool stone was rough under my hand. A vision flashed before me. Two little girls, about four years old, with brown skin and black hair, were running around this wall, laughing and playing together.

I knew immediately who they were.

Chills ran up my neck. One of the little girls was me, and the other was the angry woman spirit who had visited me in Glastonbury.

I didn't want to stand. I kept holding on to the stone wall, hoping to see more of the flashback, but it was gone. The emotion of the memory was so strong, tears streamed down my face.

I finally stood up and continued to explore. More flashbacks came. I saw where we used to sleep, where we prayed, and where we played. She and I had been best friends. We grew up in that temple. We lived in community there.

The memories were so clear and went so deep. My eyes and cheeks were wet with tears, but no sounds escaped my lips. I was trying to keep my emotions to myself, but I had an overwhelming desire to sob. *Where can I go to get away from all these people?*

As I looked around the temple for some private space, something magical happened. Suddenly, there was no one there. I called out, "Hello!" but received no answer. All of the other tourists had disappeared. I peeked along the trail, and no one was coming. I was completely alone.

Without thinking too much about how this might have happened, I moved quickly, knowing that I had a brief window of solitude in the temple. I found a big stone to sit on, and with relief, I let the sobs pour out. I wasn't sure exactly why I was crying, but I couldn't hold it back.

I felt a desire to invite the angry woman spirit to be

with me. My heart was beating wildly again, and for a few seconds, I battled with myself. *Why call her in?* I had never called in an angry spirit before. But something inside me knew she needed to be there. *What am I going to say? What if she comes and spoils this wondrous experience?*

My sobs were shaking my body now as I held the intention for her to come.

She came. I could see her in front of me now, and not just in my periphery. But she wasn't flesh and blood like me. She was transparent. It was easier to see her when I held her in soft focus. Her face wasn't angry any more. Long, straight, black hair flowed down her back. She was wearing a light brown tunic with shiny clips, or ornaments. She was a slim, strong build and I wondered if she was a warrior.

I had the sense that something had happened between us, something very painful.

"I betrayed you didn't I?" I ask her in my mind. She nodded.

Memories of a long-forgotten time came to me. When we grew up, we both became strong leaders in the community. She made a decision about something. It was a big decision, and I had disagreed. Instead of challenging her and talking things through, I decided to leave. This was a drastic choice, as it meant leaving behind everything I loved—my family, my community, the temple—never to return, until now.

After I left, the community turned on her and blamed her for my departure.

The parallels with my leaving Martin weren't lost on me.

Putting myself in her shoes, I could only imagine what it might have been like for her having her best friend walk away and then having others blame her for it. My body shook with emotion, feeling her hurt and anger.

I thought of Miriam and Emily and I cried even harder, feeling her pain as well as my own.

Through my sobs I whispered, "Please forgive me."

She nodded.

I sat there for a moment until my tears subsided. There were still no tourists around. Feeling it was time to move, I got up and stood in front of the temple taking in a deep breath. To my surprise, my breathing came easily. My nose was no longer blocked. My heart felt light, as if a dark, heavy cloud had lifted. Moving my body to check that what I was experiencing was real, I noticed that my body was no longer tired. In fact, the heat didn't bother me at all! I felt fantastic!

I began to giggle and realised I hadn't heard myself laugh for days.

Has an old memory of hurt been harboured in my heart all this time? And have I just now set it free?

I felt so much gratitude. I thanked the temple for bringing those memories back to me, and I thanked my friend for her courage to forgive. I could feel her presence, but I could no longer see her.

I took my time walking along the path back to the bus. I wanted to linger in the experience a bit longer and allow all of it to sink in. It was almost as if I was in a happy state of shock. I could barely feel my feet touch the ground. My breathing was clear and easy, as I took in the warm sea air. My body felt alive and well and happy.

Then, suddenly, my mind kicked in. *What just happened? Was that real?* But how could I question the validity of what had just happened? The memories had been so vivid, and the difference in my body was extreme, not to mention the euphoria I felt.

As I walked back into the information kiosk on my way out to the bus, I looked for the old man behind the counter. He saw me and pulled down his glasses. For a moment our eyes connected in that space of remembering beyond our words. I smiled. He smiled. "Did you find what you were looking for?"

I nodded. What else could I say? The memory of what I had just experienced quickly flooded back, and I felt the tears not far away.

He smiled again, and turned to speak with the tourist waiting in front of his desk.

As I made my way to the bus I decided to take myself out for a special dinner that evening, to celebrate what had been a strange and wonderful day. Telepathically, I reached out to my friend back at the temple and invited her to join me, but I didn't get a response.

I wondered if she was going to show up.

Chapter 19

"Table for one," I said to the dark-haired man who greeted me. *Well, maybe for two, but you won't see my friend if she comes.*

I chose a popular Italian restaurant not far from where I was staying. Once I was seated, I pulled out my coloured pens and paper and placed them on the table. I wanted to document what had happened at the temple.

"Would you like something to drink, madam?" Another dark-haired man gave me the menu and wandered off with my order for a glass of red wine.

My eyes explored the tasteful surroundings. Dark red velvet drapes hung gracefully from the ceiling, and colourful paintings and elaborately-framed mirrors decorated the walls. The beauty of the décor nourished me.

My hand reached up to touch my shoulder. My skin was a bit chilled from the air conditioning, and the tip of my nose was cold, too. I was surprised to find myself craving the natural warm air of the outdoors.

Then, suddenly, she was there, sitting in the chair across from me. I was thrilled to see her.

"Are you ready to order, madam?" the waiter asked, taking me by surprise.

It felt strange ordering food and not asking her if she wanted anything. *But what if she does want something?*

How will that work? Should I order an extra plate and then just leave it untouched in front of what would look to the waiter like an empty chair?

I ordered a salad and some spaghetti and hoped that she wouldn't be offended. When the waiter left, my attention returned fully to her. She wasn't smiling, but I didn't pick up any bad feelings. She just watched me intently.

I could tell she wasn't going to start the conversation, so I asked, "Would you like to talk about what happened?" I was curious to find out more about our lives in the temple, and this was a great opportunity.

She shook her head and gestured with her hands as if to say, "That's in the past. It's over." Then she spoke to me telepathically, the same way I had spoken to her. "I want to know what you have been up to," she said. Her tone was very determined.

"Your salad, madam." The waiter placed the plate in front of me. He startled me again. *That's right, I ordered some food.*

"Do you want anything to eat?" I asked her in my mind, feeling a bit foolish, but she ignored my question. She had quite a warrior spirit, I sensed. I wondered if we had been warriors together.

I moved some lettuce leaves around with my fork. I needed time to think how I was going to answer her question. It was so huge. *Where do I start, and do I even have an answer for her?*

I started sharing with her about my life in this lifetime. I felt her becoming agitated. At first I thought maybe I wasn't telling her what she wanted to hear. But my intuition told me she was realising how much time she had wasted by staying stuck in her own anger and spite.

She wasn't really interested in my life. She wanted to move on in hers.

My heart opened with compassion for her. I stopped sharing about myself and said, "This process of life is not a linear one. You don't have to follow the same path I took. Your journey continues from where you are in this moment."

The sense of urgency I felt from her dissipated, and her face softened.

I could feel our time together was ending. I knew she wanted to move on. She offered to not go right away and to stay to help me for the rest of my visit in Malta, so that I wouldn't get lost again. I laughed, wondering if she had really contributed to my getting so lost when I first arrived. In the end, I decided it didn't matter. I felt her care for me now.

Some part of me wanted her to stay close by. We had only just found each other again, and I would have loved to have more time with her. But I didn't want to hold her back. I knew the highest thing for me to do was to let her go.

"I think you have a far more important journey waiting for you," I said.

The waiter arrived then with my spaghetti. "Would you like anything else madam?" "No. I have everything I need," I said to him, to her and to myself. He walked away, leaving the two of us to continue our conversation.

I knew that once I had said the words I was about to say, I would never see her again. Tears filled my eyes as I spoke. "There are lights all around you now," I said. "They look like stars. Can you see them?" She nodded, and I continued. "They will take you, whenever you are ready, on the next part of your journey. Go with them."

As soon as I finished my last sentence she started to shimmer and become more and more transparent. Then she was gone.

"Goodbye," I whispered out loud. I closed my eyes and felt the grief of our parting. When I opened my eyes I spoke to an empty chair, "Thank you."

We had set each other free, just like Miriam and I had.

I wished Emily and I could meet like this.

The morning of the day I left Malta, I stood in front of a seven-foot-high wooden gate. I was surprised to see a sign that said "Garden Café—OPEN." I had walked by that gate several times during my stay, and each time it said "Garden Café—CLOSED."

The closed gate revealed nothing about what was behind it. The wood was old and worn, and hadn't seen a lick of paint or stain. I lifted the rusty latch, pushed the gate open and stepped inside. My mouth hung open as I looked at the garden oasis before me. Trees, bushes and colourful flowers were everywhere. Lush green grass carpeted the entire area. Water gently trickled from a fountain. And as if by an artist's brush strokes on canvas, white wicker chairs and tables with gazebos and marquees were dotted about the grounds.

I looked back towards the street, knowing it was dry and barren on the other side of the gate. I shook my head. *This was only around the corner from me the whole time.*

A small blackboard advertised scones and coffee— exactly what I wanted. Nestling into one of the comfortable wicker chairs, I pulled out my coloured pens and note book. "Would you like to look at the menu?" the waitress asked with a smile.

"No, thanks. I'll have an espresso and a scone."

"I'm sorry but we don't have any scones. The chef makes them for the afternoon. Would you like something else?"

Oh darn. I was so looking forward to that scone. "No, thanks. I'll just have the coffee." *I don't really need a scone anyway.*

The waitress came back with my coffee. "The chef is making you some fresh scones. I'll bring them over when they are ready."

"Thank you so much! And please thank the chef, too." Now I really was in heaven.

I was enjoying my coffee and scones when a man and woman approached. They had been sitting at another table in the garden. "Excuse me," the man said. "They put your coffee on my bill by mistake, and I paid for it. I wanted you to know that I wanted to do that."

Without another word, they both smiled and walked out of the café.

For a couple of seconds I was speechless. What do you say to someone you don't know who has just done something so thoughtful? Tears of gratitude filled my eyes. I felt so loved by life. It was only a coffee. It was only a scone. But it meant so much.

"Oh, my. Thank you!" I managed to call out after them.

How strange to have faced so many challenges, not to mention an angry spirit from a past life, only to find myself now sitting in what felt like the Garden of Eden having all my wishes granted.

When I first arrived in Malta, I thought that the angels had left me. But it was actually me who had left them. It was me who had stopped listening. It was only when I'd had enough of my own misery that I started to listen to my intuition again.

Had my journey ended then, I would have been completely satisfied.

But it wasn't over yet.

Chapter 20

I sat on the edge of the bed in a tiny motel room close to London's Gatwick Airport. My itinerary was spread out before me as I went over my flights for the next morning.

The window was wide open. It was a warm night, but remembering the cool weather in Glastonbury only two weeks before, I looked at the thin blanket folded at the end of the bed. *I hope this is going to keep me warm tonight.* I pulled it over my legs.

I looked around the room. Bare, beige walls, no furniture apart from a small double bed and two cubes used as bedside tables. Nothing else would have fit. This was a definite downgrade from my large, exotic room in Malta, but it fit my needs perfectly since I had an early morning flight.

Even though I had already looked over my itinerary, I peered through the papers again and saw something that I hadn't seen, until now, in the light of a bit more experience: there was only a two-hour gap between my arrival in Philadelphia and my departure to New York. I studied the map of the Philadelphia airport that my travel agent had given me. I was arriving on an international flight and needed to transfer to a domestic flight which left from Terminal F. Terminal F was the farthest terminal from the one I would arrive at.

I recalled my travel agent pointing this out back in

New Zealand. "Do you want me to change that, Leanne? I could put you on another flight, but it will mean flying out the day before and staying a night in Philadelphia."

Being an inexperienced traveller, I thought that two hours would be plenty. Blindly confident, I said, "No, that's okay."

But as I sat on the bed in my motel room the night before the flight, I understood my mistake. I had met enough travellers with stories of extensive security measures and the need for extra time when flying through the United States to know that two hours would not be enough.

I had been so excited about registering for The Shadow Process weekend course where I planned to face my inner demons and ultimately make peace with myself. This was a key part of my pilgrimage and if I missed the flight then I would miss the first day of the programme and would probably have to forfeit the whole thing.

Have I come all this way and spent all this money only to miss the course? I was angry with myself for not having taken an extra day to travel to New York, and I felt anxious knowing that I was going to have to deal with unknown consequences now.

Just then, a breeze blew in the window and took my attention away from my growing panic. I stood up to close the window, and in that moment of interruption, I remembered: whatever happened was the journey. If I missed my flight and missed the course then I would be wherever I was supposed to be. It would be some other adventure, and it would be the adventure I was meant to be on.

All my anger and anxiety disappeared, and a soothing calm began to flow in my chest. I closed my eyes and counted my breaths, making sure I was breathing evenly. The calmness grew. Then I did the only thing I knew to do. I asked the divine forces in charge of miracles for help. With my eyes still closed, I called in the angels and I brought into my vision all of the flight paths on my itinerary for the next day. I imagined them filling with bright, white light, and they filled easily, with no breaks.

This was interesting. I had done this ritual before, and if there were going to be any disruptions, I would have expected some breaks in the light. I interpreted this to mean that I was going to make my flight just fine. *But how?*

"Am I going to make my flight?" I asked the angels—just to check.

"Yes," came the response.

"Will you help me make my flight?"

"We're working on it."

I opened my eyes and folded up my papers. My intuition was all I had to go on, and chances were already high that I would miss the flight, so I had nothing to lose.

A strong urge guided me to pack some overnight things into my carry-on bag. I had never done that before. My fingers shook as I put the few extra items into my knapsack. *Why am I doing this? Am I going to be separated from my luggage? I can't afford to lose it. It has everything I need for the next five weeks and some of my favourite clothes.*

The anxious feelings had returned.

I knew I had to interrupt my fearful thoughts in order to calm myself. I began to hum a little tune as I continued to rearrange the items in my bags. As long as I was moving and focusing my attention on what I was doing, I couldn't think.

In no time, my bags were ready and standing by the door, which was the only space for them in my tiny room. I put myself to bed and went straight to sleep.

The alarm went off just before dawn. Opening my eyes, I reminded myself, "This *is* the journey." All of my senses were alert, but I still felt relaxed.

We arrived in Philadelphia on time. Going through customs and immigration was smooth. I picked up my luggage from the carousel and looked at my watch. Thirty minutes to get to my connecting flight. It was possible. My spirits were high.

The woman at the check-in counter for connecting flights retagged my bag and handed it back to me. I thought I was leaving it with her, but she shook her head. She told me I needed to take my bag somewhere else. This was when things started to go wrong.

When she told me where to take my bag, it was as if cotton wool had been stuffed in my ears. I could not understand what she was saying. She was an English-speaking American and was speaking clear English to me, but her words sounded jumbled in my brain. I shook my head, thinking maybe I had brain fog from the long flight. *I don't have time for this to happen.*

I asked her to repeat what she was saying three more

times. She spoke slowly and clearly, pointing to where I needed to go, but each time I could not make any sense from her words. My distress was rising.

Behind me was a growing line of people with flights to catch. I couldn't bear to ask her one more time, so I stepped away from the counter. I didn't realise it then, but I wasn't meant to understand her.

I decided to go slowly and to take things one step at a time. I breathed deeply into my chest and let go of trying to figure things out. I had nothing to go on now but trust that the next step would appear.

I did understand from what she said that I had to take my suitcase to the big X-ray machine behind me in the middle of the airport hall. I placed my luggage on the conveyor belt and went to the other end of the machine, where I stood watching the comings and goings of travellers and wondering what I needed to do next.

A security man walking briskly past looked at me and asked, "Are you going to Terminal F?" There were many people in the airport going to many different destinations. *Why has he singled me out?*

"Yes," I said.

He continued at his hasty pace, "It's this way," motioning for me to follow.

"But the woman at the counter was pointing over there," I said, indicating the opposite direction. He shrugged and kept going.

I had a split second to decide if I was going to follow him or not as he began to disappear down the hall. My whole body wanted to follow, and so without another thought I dashed after him. The top of his hat was all I could see above the heads of so many people and soon he was lost in the crowds, but I began to see airport signs saying "Terminal F." Things were looking good.

In my spontaneity, however, I forgot about my suitcase and any thought of it had completely abandoned my mind.

Still following the signs for Terminal F, I headed down a long corridor. There was still no trace of the security guard but that didn't matter. The airport signs were clear now. I glanced at my watch. Twenty minutes to go. I was going to make it.

Finally there was a big sign saying "Terminal F" pointing to the left. Clearly I was getting closer.

My body began to relax. Even though I had told myself that this was the journey, there was always a slight undercurrent of tension and wondering, *Will I make the flight? Will I get there on time?* Finally I could let that all go.

When I reached the sign, I looked to the left where it indicated. There before me were at least a hundred other people milling around waiting. This wasn't Terminal F. This was the boarding area for the shuttle taking people to the different terminals. All of these people needed to go through security before they boarded the shuttle.

My heart sank. I wasn't going to make it. Just out of curiosity, I asked someone how long the shuttle ride to Terminal F took. "Thirty minutes," he replied. I estimated it would take approximately an hour and a half to get to the terminal from where I was.

My knapsack was getting heavy on my back. I took it

off and reached for my water bottle. I reminded myself that this was the journey. Whatever happened next was supposed to happen. I felt surprisingly calm and alert. *Everything is going to be okay, wherever I end up.* Taking a sip of water, I felt my body relax as I searched for the next step.

"I need your help," I whispered to the angels.

I scanned the people packed into the shuttle boarding area and met the eyes of another security guard about eight metres away from me. He kept his eyes on me as he said, "Is anyone going to Terminal F?" I looked around expecting a sea of hands to go up, but none did. Everyone kept talking or doing whatever they were doing as if he hadn't spoken. It was as if they hadn't heard him.

I raised my hand and he motioned for me to approach him. Looking at my ticket, he said, "You're not going to make your flight if you stay here. If you want, you can go down those stairs, go outside and catch the employees' shuttle to Terminal F. You'll get there on time, and you can go through security there."

My heart was racing, and my mind was full of questions. *Is this really happening? Aren't there other people here for Terminal F? Why didn't anyone else hear him?*

For a brief moment, doubts flooded my mind. *What if I get lost? What if they won't let me onto the shuttle? What if I get caught being where I am not supposed to be? Maybe I should stay here. At least I know what will happen if I stay.*

I was being offered a miracle, and my fear was trying to keep me safe. Luckily, I didn't deliberate too long.

Tossing my fears aside like an old tissue, I told the man that he was an angel and dashed down the stairs. I was going to make my flight! I was going to make it to the course! I was elated.

Within ten minutes, I had reached Terminal F, and just on time.

It wasn't until I was standing alone in front of an empty luggage carousel at New York's Stewart Airport that it finally dawned on me that I had left my suitcase behind in Philadelphia, probably in the middle of the floor at the end of the X-ray machine.

My stomach turned. *How could I have done that?* In my mind I could hear the automated message drone from the airport loudspeakers. "If you see any un-attended baggage, call security immediately." I saw disturbing visions of my luggage being blown up by airport security. I felt sad and disappointed imagining all the precious things inside my suitcase being destroyed. *Well if that is what happened, then it was supposed to happen. What's the point of getting upset?*

Waiting in the lost luggage queue, I mentally went through the items in my bag, letting each one go. This process was going smoothly until I remembered the gorgeous blue dress I had bought in Glastonbury. *Oh darn. I'd hate to lose that one.* I frowned.

Finally I reached the front of the queue. The young man behind the counter looked tired and overworked, and he didn't even look at me as he began his robotic spiel. "Yes, ma'am. I'm sorry we lost your luggage. What's your flight number?"

His fingers were poised above the computer keys waiting for the number.

"Actually, you didn't lose my luggage," I said. "I did something really silly." He looked up from his keyboard while I told him what I did. As I spoke, his eyes opened wider. He sat up straight and smiled as if to say, "I haven't heard this one before." His eyebrows furrowed with concern.

"Let's see what we can do," he said, punching my ticket number into his keyboard. After a few seconds he said, "I've found your luggage."

I was ecstatic, but for a moment I felt a bit confused. I had just spent all that time letting it all go. What did it matter if he had found it or not? Apart from the dress. Well, I guess letting it go was not the same as losing it. If I could let it all go and not have to lose it, that would be fantastic.

"It's in San Diego."

What is it doing over there? Even more intriguing was the fact that it was not with airport security. Someone, some angel, must have picked it up and boarded it on a flight. That meant there was now a good chance that I would get it back.

But now I had a different concern.

Looking directly into the young man's eyes, I said, "I know my luggage will find its way back here, because that's your job. But I am here for only two days on a course and then I fly to Arizona. If it doesn't get here within the two days, I'm not sure it will find me." I paused for a moment. The next part of my trip was with a shaman in Sedona. I didn't want to spend that time hanging around Phoenix waiting for my bag. There was still a chance I might lose it.

It was also a Friday. I knew there would probably be fewer staff working on the weekend, so it might take longer than usual for my luggage to be retrieved. "If my luggage were to get here by the end of this weekend, I know that would take a lot of extra effort on your part," I said. "I want you to know that I know that."

As I stood there holding his gaze, I felt a lot of compassion for him. He seemed to be either bored or just very tired, and the last thing he needed was a lot of extra work.

After a few seconds in silence, I sighed and let go of my luggage once again. If I got it back, I got it back. If I didn't, I didn't. It was all in his hands. There was nothing more I could do. In my mind, I whispered, "Angels, please help him."

"Leave it with me, ma'am." And so I did.

Chapter 21

I wandered out of the airport to find a shuttle to my hotel. I was tired, but I also felt lighter inside, maybe simply because I didn't have a heavy suitcase to carry.

I put my knapsack on the seat beside me, and patted it, grateful I had filled it with some extra overnight things from my suitcase. I took in a deep breath and smiled as a shiver of excitement went through me. *Who would have thought the day would have unfolded like this?*

As the shuttle gently bounced and swayed its way to the hotel, I started to laugh. Here I was on my way to participate in a personal development course, and I had already let go of my 'baggage.' My course had begun.

The hotel was small and the décor was dated. The large-flower-patterned wallpaper in the lounge and bar area was probably the fashion in the nineteen-eighties. Old dark brown velvet curtains hung lifelessly and the worn, drab, brown carpet needed replacing. But it was clean and well-kept and near the airport which was exactly what I needed, as the shuttle bound for the Omega Institute would pick me up there in the morning.

My room was just like the rest of the hotel—clean, well-kept and dated.

The following morning, I boarded the Omega Institute shuttle. A vivacious woman with long blond hair sat in the seat facing me. "Where are you from?"

"Ohio," she said with a smile. "And what about you, where do you live?"

Lorriane and I were filled with questions for each other as we discovered how many things we had in common. We both spoke French, her birthday was also in August, we both had blonde hair, she was attending the same course as me, and we had both lost a piece of luggage on our way!

Lorriane was a coach, too. I wondered how many clients she had. *From what she says it sounds like she's really good. Is she a better coach than me?* I noticed how she spoke with so much ease and confidence, and I wondered if I came across like that. That familiar feeling of inadequacy began to rise, but I pushed it away.

"My partner and I are working out our living circumstances," she said, frowning. "He lives in Italy, so we travel back and forth a lot. It's hard. I'd love to move there, but right now I'm staying in Ohio to be with my son." Just the mention of her son made her smile, and again I felt inadequate for not having any children of my own.

I took a deep breath, and pushing away my own feelings I felt into Lorriane's situation and felt compassion for her. I smiled and put my hand on her hand.

"Excuse me," the man sitting beside me leaned in closer. "You two look like you are having a good connection, and I hope I'm not interrupting. My name is Brent and I'm attending The Shadow Process, too."

We were very happy to greet another fellow

participant. Brent shared that he and his second wife were talking about separating, but he didn't want to break up. He suspected he had been sabotaging his relationships for a long time, and wanted to get to the bottom of it on the course.

His determination and courage moved me. For a moment I wondered if Martin would have been willing to... but I let the thought go.

The three of us continued to share our own life stories and our reasons for being at The Shadow Process, and I felt a close kinship with them both. When we arrived at the venue, we parted ways, planning to catch up during the course that evening.

After checking in at the reception area, I went outside to take in my surroundings. The Omega Institute, located in Rhinebeck, New York, was like an eco-village with café, library, shops, spa and more, all housed in simple wooden buildings framed by tasteful gardens and landscaping. The photos I saw on the Internet were nothing compared to seeing it in person.

I am finally here.

My mind cast back to my cabin on the farm. That's where I was when I saw the video of Debbie Ford talking about the Shadow Process. I was so inspired that I paused the video and did an Internet search for when and where the next courses would be, knowing they would be impossibly far away and out of my reach financially. I was right.

I'll do it someday, I thought, knowing that I never would. If my shadow had had a persona, it would have been rubbing its hands and chuckling at its own success in holding me back.

But it hadn't held me back for long. I had made it, and in a couple of hours, the course would begin. I stomped each foot to feel the soles of my feet on the ground. This was real. I closed my eyes as they welled with tears of gratitude, for all the miracles that had conspired, and for the courage it had taken me to find myself standing here—from buying my ticket, to listening to my intuition, leaving my bag behind, and making my flight.

I breathed in deeply. *I am here.*

After exploring the area, I took a moment to settle into my room. It was one of twelve rooms in a dormitory with shared kitchen and washroom facilities. A single bed was against the wall by the window, and a three-drawer dresser against the other wall. *I won't need that. I don't have anything to put in it.* I smiled and placed my notebook and pen on the table by the bed.

The course was beginning soon and usually I would have spent time thinking about what to wear, but without my suitcase, I had no options. It felt rather liberating. I looked down at my top—the same top I had worn the day before—and my hand brushed it as if smoothing out a wrinkle. I wondered if I would feel self-conscious wearing the same thing every day, but I reminded myself that people would be busy dealing with their shadows, not scrutinizing my clothes.

I stepped outside into the dusk and the freshness of the evening dew filled my lungs. My skin tingled. I pulled my shawl around my shoulders and snuggled into it. It wasn't chilly, I just felt like hugging myself.

As the evening darkened, the solar powered lampposts and fairy lights along the pathways brightened, creating an enchanted wonderland. I followed them all the way to the auditorium. The hum of voices from several hundred people gathering around the theatre grew louder as I approached. Lorriane and I spotted each other, and like two excited teenagers on the first day of school, our voices joined the buzz of chatter.

As I entered the room I was conscious of the slight ache in my belly from nervous feelings of anticipation. It was like being on the slow, uphill part of a rollercoaster. You know that you are okay, but only for a few more seconds, because very soon you will reach the peak and start heading downwards—fast.

The thrill of freedom and the fear of losing control.

I squeezed my hands together and walked in. *Here I go.*

Over the next couple of days, I dove into the depths of the darkness inside myself. The questions the course asked were powerful, and they went directly to the core of my pain, shame, regret, suffering and dishonesty.

Initially I thought, *I don't have much of a shadow. I've already done a lot of work on myself. I feel healthy and strong, and I'm in a good place right now.* But that was just my ego trying to keep me on the surface, avoiding the downhill-out-of-control part.

As I let go, the drawers of the filing cabinets holding memories stored in the depths of my being were pulled wide open.

One of the questions the course asked was about pain

or suffering I had caused others. My mind flashed back to my third grade teacher, Miss Stanley. She was always patient and kind, she explained things in a way I could understand, and I regarded her highly and enjoyed being in her class. She also had a deformity that made her back crooked and one of her legs shorter than the other.

That year, I was seated beside Mike, one of the class bullies. He was a big guy for an eight year old. He hadn't picked on me before, but I knew that I could easily become one of his targets. I had already been bullied by a group of girls. They threatened to beat me up and waited for me outside the school, and I had to stay behind in the classroom until they all gave up and went home. I didn't want that to happen again.

I was wondering what to do to get on Mike's good side, and one day while Miss Stanley was talking with the class about taking a field trip to the beach, I decided to try and be funny and make him laugh. Leaning over to Mike, I whispered a comment about seeing Miss Stanley in a bathing suit.

As soon as the words came out of my mouth, remorse coursed through my veins, but my plan had worked—the bully laughed. Miss Stanley wanted to know what I had said to make him laugh so much, but I couldn't tell her. She kept me after class that day and asked me again, but I stayed silent. Every cell of my being was drowning in shame. Tears of anguish stung my eyes as I sat there looking down at the floor.

I remembered other things, things I hadn't thought about in years. I remembered when I was thirteen and an old man called out to me for help, but I ran away because I was scared. I remembered the time I let myself run out of money and couldn't afford to buy food, so I stopped eating. I recalled the many times I had wanted to say, "No!" but didn't when men touched me in places I didn't want them to.

I remembered the hearts I had broken, the selfish actions I had taken that hurt others, the actions I hadn't taken to stand up for myself and for what was right, and the lies I had told to myself and others to cover my mistakes.

All these parts of myself came to the surface, and I felt shame, guilt, anger, sadness and helplessness. The pain was deep. A part of me wanted to run away. I wanted to say, *That was just a bad day. I'm not like that now. I was so young then. I didn't really know what I was doing. That happened so long ago. It doesn't really matter now does it?*

But it did matter. I had come here to face the things I hated myself for, no matter how big or small anyone else thought they were. I had come to face my shadow. I was not going to run away from her. I was going to stay right there and be with her, admit to her, and put my arms around her.

At some point during one of the exercises, I think it was after I had used up a whole box of tissues crying about some situation or another, the thing I was crying about suddenly seemed completely trivial. I had gone to the bottom of the barrel, there was nowhere else to go, and now being at the bottom it didn't seem so bad.

I stopped crying. There was peace inside me. It was

as if there had been a war going on around me, and all of a sudden it had stopped. I saw how much drama and significance I had generated around things that now seemed hardly to matter at all.

I had created the war, and I had just ended it.

I began to laugh at the theatrics of it all. Looking down at the fistful of soggy, used tissues I had been clutching desperately in my hand, I laughed even harder and dropped them to the floor.

As I continued with the course, I began to see that it wasn't about getting rid of these parts of myself that were hard to face. It was about discovering their gifts. I realised that being needy brought me the gift of being sensitive and loving. Being disorganised and chaotic brought me the gift of being a free spirit. Being afraid brought me the gift of courage. Being insecure brought me the gift of trusting myself.

I couldn't have just one side of the coin. The key was to embrace it all, the good and the bad, and to own it.

During our breaks, Lorriane, Brent and I caught each other's eyes and smiled, hugged and sometimes shared a meal or a cup of tea.

On Saturday afternoon, I saw Brent sitting under a tree, so I headed his way. "Mind if I join you?"

"I'd love it if you did," he said, managing a smile.

I sat down beside him. "How is the course going for you?"

"I've just realised why Heather gets so angry with me."

"I'm listening."

"Whenever I'm feeling down, maybe something happened at work, or I just feel down about myself, I tell Heather that she's too good for me. What I really mean is she is so intelligent, together and beautiful, I wonder how she could possibly love a schmuck like me."

I thought about Martin. He had never actually said anything like that, but he often used to walk two feet behind me. It was strange, and I didn't like it. In fact, sometimes I got really annoyed. I tried several strategies to change it, but none worked. When I pointed it out to him, he said he wasn't aware of it. I wondered if maybe subconsciously he thought he wasn't good enough.

"Then she gets really mad," Brent continued. "We end up fighting, threatening to leave each other. I could never figure out how we kept getting into the same awful argument until now. When I feel down and not worthy, that's my shadow. I can't be with someone loving me, because I am not loving myself. I hate that part of myself. So I pretty much tell her she should leave me." He looked down at the ground. He pulled out some blades of grass, and letting out a big sigh he leaned back and looked at the sky.

I thought about when I didn't want to buy the orchard and let it go ahead anyway. As I zoomed in closer to myself in that moment, I believed that my voice did not have an equal right to be heard. I felt small and helpless. That must have been awful for Martin to be with. He did not have a full partner in purchasing that property.

My attention moved back to Brent. "That's a powerful

insight," I said. "What will you do now?"

"I'm going to go back and share all of this with her. Hopefully now that I'm more conscious of it, I can make better choices in the moment."

We sat in silence reflecting on our own inner worlds and feeling each other's support.

As I continued to peel open the gifts of my shadow, I found it had great wisdom to share. As I embraced all of me, the good and the bad, I began to feel whole and strong, less judgmental of myself and others, more free to speak my truth. A feeling of peace and aliveness permeated my being.

By the end of the course, Lorriane, Brent and I knew we would be life-long friends, having bared our deepest regrets and our most painful wounds together. As we shared with each other on the shuttle ride back to the airport, our voices were strong, clear, and heartfelt— very different from the nervous and excited chatter of our first meeting.

"I've registered for their coach training," Lorriane said.

"How inspiring!" I said, feeling truly excited for her. *She will be an even more outstanding coach with these tools.* I beamed love at her.

I felt so peaceful and present with both of them as we spoke. There was no undercurrent of unease anywhere inside of me. My mind was silent. I was at peace within myself. I knew my shadow wasn't gone. The course wasn't about making it go away. But in that moment, I no longer needed to be ashamed of it or pretend it wasn't there.

With hugs, tears and promises to keep in touch, we each went our own way—them to the airport and me back to my clean, well-kept and dated hotel for one more night. The next day, I was flying to Arizona to spend six days on a shamanic vision quest.

"Booking for Leanne Babcock," I said to the woman behind the desk at the hotel. She smiled and said, "We have your luggage, Miss Babcock."

There behind her was my suitcase with a very large red sticker on it saying "URGENT."

In my mind, I saw the young man's face at the lost luggage counter as he said, "Leave it with me, ma'am." I smiled a big smile and held the image of his face in my mind as I said out loud, "Thank you."

"You're welcome," said the woman behind the counter, and I smiled even more.

As I wheeled my suitcase to my room, I noticed that everything looked magnificent and vibrant. Nothing looked dated or drab, not even the old, plain, faded carpet. Its colour was a lush, deep chocolaty-brown with different velvety textures. There was nothing plain about it.

My soul felt fully nourished as I fell into a blissful night's sleep.

Chapter 22

The sun was already setting in Phoenix by the time my flight landed. *Hello Arizona.* I excitedly peered out the plane window, trying to see as much as I could.

My plans in Arizona were taking shape. The night before, in my chocolate-carpeted hotel room, I'd had a Skype call with Lisa to tell her how The Shadow Process had gone. We'd both shared deeply about our experiences, and before ending our call, Lisa mentioned a spiritual conference in Tucson she thought I might be interested in. She told me it was a four-day international event which would include meditations, healing sessions, talks and music. She wanted to go herself but had already committed to something else.

As soon as I hung up, I searched for the "World Congress on Illumination" online and discovered that the timing of the event was ideal. It started nine days after my vision quest ended, which meant I could attend the first two days before flying to Canada to visit with Mom. The nine days between the vision quest and the congress would give me just enough time to visit the Grand Canyon and process my experiences while spending several days alone in a cabin in the woods. It was perfect.

Standing in the queue to pick up my rental car, I fidgeted with the papers in my hand. It will be dark soon. I didn't like driving in the dark and particularly on the side of the road I was unaccustomed to. I had learned to drive in New Zealand.

"Would you like a GPS?" the man behind the counter asked me. "Yes please." I had no intention of repeating the Malta driving experience! It was a two-hour drive to Sedona, and that GPS was going to be my best friend in the dark.

"You're in luck. This is our last one." I looked at the queue of people behind me. *You're kidding. What are these people going to do?* I quickly returned my attention to myself and was grateful that I got it.

I slid tentatively into the driver's seat and put my right hand on the gear shift. My left hand felt helpless on the steering wheel, feeling like it should be doing something else. Both of my hands shook a little. *Why do I put myself in these challenging situations? I could have taken a different flight and made sure I arrived in the daytime, so at least I wouldn't have to do this in the dark.*

I mentally shifted gears. *You can do this, Leanne. Other people do it all the time. You have a map, you have a GPS, and it's a fairly straight road. So what if it takes you three hours to get there.* I looked at my watch. It was nine o'clock.

"Keep to the right. Keep to the right," I chanted to myself as I pulled out of the parking lot.

"In five hundred feet turn right," the voice of the GPS was soothing. Driving further away from the city lights, the darkness of the night began to close in around my headlights, and the stretch of highway before me was reduced to several metres.

I had a long straight stretch before me. Glancing

at the GPS, I was comforted by its light.

Strangely, there were almost no other cars on the road going either way. It was eerie. *It would be awful to break down here.* I quickly moved my attention back to the road.

In my peripheral vision, the light of the GPS flickered and then went out. Reaching over I pressed the restart button. Nothing. I pulled over and proceeded to press every possible button that might be helpful. *Don't panic, Leanne. Keep breathing. You can figure this out.* But the GPS was dead.

I stared at it, desperately hoping that some life would appear. *This can't be happening. I did everything to make sure I was not going to get lost this time.*

I tried to tell myself that "this *is* the journey," but I wasn't listening. Terror was already pumping through my veins. But I had a map and a piece of paper with the directions to where I was staying. I took a few deep, slow breaths and calmed down when I read the instructions. They sounded simple enough, but the test would be in following them.

I drove in silence in the dark.

At the end of the highway, there was a junction where I had a choice of three roads: left, right or straight ahead up a ramp that crossed back over the highway. The map said this was Sedona, but I couldn't see any city lights. It looked just as deserted and dark as the highway. The one street lamp lighting the junction left all of the street signs in the dark.

The directions said turn left at Bear Canyon.

Looking at the road signs that I couldn't read in the

dark, I shook my head. *How does anyone find their way at night here?*

I looked all around. There were no other cars. I manoeuvred the car to read each street sign with the headlights. None of them said Bear Canyon.

Instead of giving in to fear, I decided to use my intuition. I asked myself which way felt right to me, but I didn't get a clear answer, so I took the road to the left. After driving a short distance, something inside of me didn't feel right. I turned around and took the road leading up the ramp. After a couple of minutes, I saw a sign for Bear Canyon. I took in a nice long breath and relaxed.

From there my accommodation was easy to find. I looked at my watch as I pulled into the driveway. Almost midnight. *Yep, three hours.* I smiled.

I quickly settled in and went to bed, but I couldn't sleep. I had a meeting at five-thirty in the morning with Kimberley, the shaman I would be working with for the rest of the week. My mind raced ahead to the morning, when I would have to find my way with no street map and no GPS. *What if I get lost? What if others are kept waiting? I have no way of reaching her.*

I had intentionally not brought my cell phone as I didn't want to deal with any matters from back in New Zealand, but it also meant I didn't have a way to be in communication with people here. I decided to handle that and get a small prepaid cell phone at some point over the next couple of days.

What if I'm late? Will she wait?

"Oh shut up," I said out loud. Finally the thoughts were silent, and I drifted off into a short, light sleep.

My alarm went off. I peered out the window, but it was still dark outside. *So this is Sedona.* I was staying in a bedsit, in a private home and healing centre. I felt excited to be there. I couldn't see anything, but I could feel the place. The warm, slightly oppressive desert air, even at four-thirty in the morning, felt wonderful.

My room was a good size with a very comfortable single bed, a divan, a couple of chairs and two dressers. The bed cover and curtains were matching with a pretty tiny flower pattern. Colourful red and blue cushions, picking up the colours in the tiny flowers, were placed on the divan. A small outside courtyard, with a white wrought iron table and two chairs, joined the kitchenette and my room.

The owner of the house and healing centre said no one else would be staying on the premises so I had the kitchenette to myself. From time to time she would have clients visit her in her centre but their entrance was separate to mine and so the bedsit would be private.

I wondered what Kimberley would look like. *Will she look native American?* There weren't any photos of her on her website. *Will she be wearing feathers and beads? She said we are going into the bush today. I wonder what we are going to do?* I imagined we might be doing a ceremony to mark the beginning of my six-day adventure.

By the time I was ready, it was dawn. I felt comfortable in my blue sleeveless cotton t-shirt and shorts. Looking down at my grey sneakers, I smiled. *Perfect!* The parking lot where we were meeting wasn't far way and I found it easily. Kimberley was waiting in a large, gold, four-wheel drive vehicle. It certainly wasn't new but it was very clean and looked well cared-for. Her big, grey-blonde hair was all I could see as I peeked at her while I was parking. I joined her in her vehicle and wondered how she kept her car so tidy if she carried so many passengers with the equipment she must need.

She greeted me with a big smile. She was Caucasian with a good, strong build. She wore an ordinary, brown and beige checkered shirt and beige trousers, no beads or feathers. A feather hung from her rear-view mirror though.

I would soon find out that she worked with Bear energy, and being with her was like being with a mother bear. She was gentle, but she meant business.

As we drove, I was grateful to be the passenger so I could relax and enjoy the view of the horizon, the red earth, the dry, green bushes, the twisted Juniper trees, the huge red rocks and the striking desert cactus. I loved Arizona's landscape already.

When I was in New Zealand searching for a shaman to work with, Kimberley's website spoke directly to me. She offered several different adventures, and the one that excited me most was the six-day shamanic vision quest, which included a one-night-solo in the desert with all of the wildlife—spiders, snakes, scorpions, mountain lions, coyotes and wild pigs. I read through every single testimonial, making sure that she had done this kind of thing with a lot of people and they had all come back alive.

At the time, while I was still safe in my bed in New Zealand, it had seemed like a very inspiring thing to do. Now that I was about to do it, I felt an underlying tension. I wondered if it was excitement or terror.

After about twenty minutes, we pulled onto an old dirt track and parked. There was a hill to one side and a few clumps of shrubs and trees to the other. It looked pretty deserted. Kimberley said that it wasn't one of the tourist spots and we would have some privacy there. *I guess we will need some privacy if we are going to be drumming and dancing.* But in truth I had no idea what we were going to do.

I watched as Kimberley pulled two chairs out of the back of her car and placed them beside some bushes. She indicated for me to sit down. "You are going to go on a shamanic journey," she said as she gazed off into the horizon. "Your intention is to ground yourself and to remember who you are."

To remember who I am? Have I forgotten? But I knew what she meant. This would be about going beyond my ideas of who I thought I was, to a place that my mind could not fathom.

She told me I would travel down the roots of a tree where I would meet my guide. "When I sound the drum three times like this, it means it is time to come back." She drummed three times very quickly, then she nodded and began to drum the consistent beat that guided me on my journey.

Isn't she going to tell me more? Is that all I need to know? How will I know what to do when I get there? I closed my eyes and decided to trust. The constant drumming transported my mind and opened my imagination. I began to journey.

> *Before me stood a big, old twisted Juniper tree, its branches splayed out boldly inviting me in. Without hesitating, I began to slide down its roots, which swirled around me. It was like being in a wild dream, where anything could happen. As I swirled deep into the earth, I felt safe. At the end of the roots, I landed with my feet on the ground. A Native-American man greeted me. He had long, black braided hair and wore two feathers in a band on his head. Suddenly, the band transformed into the huge headdress of a chief. He began to dance and invited me to join him. As I danced with him, he gathered me into his cloak and I became a child. After a time, he put me down and shape-shifted into an eagle. He turned to me and said, "Come!" Then he lifted up and flew. I felt afraid, because I wasn't an eagle and didn't know how to fly, but I was going to lose him if I didn't follow. So I leaped into the air, and soon I was flying by his side. As we flew, he said, "Look," and I looked all around me at the sky, the expansive view, the two mountains below.*

Then I heard the three quick drum beats. I didn't want to return. I wanted to keep flying.

> *I thanked the chief who had been my guide, found the roots of the tree again and followed them back up.*

I took my time opening my eyes, wanting to savour the feeling of being so uplifted. When I had fully come out of the vision, which felt like a short ten minutes but was actually twenty-five minutes, Kimberley and I interpreted my journey. I recalled that my intention was to ground myself and to remember who I was. The man I met was one of my guides. He was inviting me to drop my preconceived notions of who I thought I was, and what I could and couldn't do. My hesitation to fly reflected my lack of belief in myself, but when I stopped thinking and trusted, I flew. This showed me that my spirit was beyond my imagining. The final part of the message was that I must maintain an eagle perspective, high above the details. Such a vision would guide me to know what was needed in my life, and in the world.

Wow. I felt like I had just been given the key to the mystery of me.

When I returned to my room at the end of the day, I headed straight to bed without dinner or a shower. I put on my night mask to shut out the daylight—it was only six-thirty—and I pulled the bed covers over me. My body surrendered to gravity. My muscles melted. My consciousness abandoned to a deep sleep.

My shamanic journey had begun.

Chapter 23

I peeked out from the night mask, and the morning light flooded in. Closing my eyes, I lay back, adjusting to the light and stretching my well-rested body. I didn't have a dawn start today.

Still in my pyjamas, with a cup of coffee in hand, I went outside to investigate my surroundings. I hadn't yet seen where I was staying in the full light of day. I walked through the small courtyard and into the backyard of the house, and my heart skipped as I entered a beautiful, lush vegetable garden surrounded by plush green grass. I quickly kicked off my sandals and dug my toes into the ground.

While surveying the garden I noticed the biggest red dragonfly I had ever seen flying towards the bush right in front of me, about a metre away. It flew around the bush, making a full circle. *What a fascinating being. It isn't even afraid of me.*

My eyes stayed on the dragonfly as it flew around the bush a second time, following the same circle. *That's strange.* I wondered if maybe it was looking for some food. Then, to my amazement, it circled a third time around the bush.

I was spellbound. *Surely it will fly in some other direction this time.* Gripping my coffee mug tightly and holding my body absolutely still, my eyes fixed on the dragonfly. *Nah, it's not going to…* my mouth opened as it went around the bush for the fourth time. Then it turned around and flew in exactly the same circle, but in the opposite direction. It did this only once, and then it flew away.

Stunned at what I had just witnessed, I knew it was a message, but what, I didn't know.

I was keen to talk with Kimberley about it. Later that day, I parked my car outside her house for our evening session. I had expected her to live in the countryside, but Kimberley lived in a small communal neighbourhood in a recently developed suburban area. Inside her house was just like her car, clean and very tidy, but there were drums and intriguing wall hangings such as masks and woven drawings everywhere.

When I asked her about the dragonfly she told me that the dragonfly represented new life and surprise. She said the message was that four things were going to happen to me, each bringing insight and transformation. Circling once in the opposite direction was a warning sign, signalling there would be one event when I would need to keep myself vigilant and aware.

I wasn't sure I wanted to know that.

During our session Kimberley said we were going to do some healing work. "This is part of the preparation for your solo-night," she said. I quivered thinking about it. "Who are you still holding anger or resentment towards?"

She doesn't waste any time.

"My ex-husband," I said, remembering the last two

months on the orchard and the pain I had felt. It was like an old movie that I had watched many times already. She didn't ask me anything else, so I didn't say any more.

She looked at me with no expression on her face. "In a moment you are going to do an emotional release healing process. I want you to call in Jaguar spirit."

Immediately I saw a black panther in my mind. The jaguar or panther spirit animal, she told me, was about meeting your fears and reclaiming your power. "You are going to walk in Jaguar's body, shaking this rattle. At the same time, you will breathe in all of the bad energy you have sent to your ex-husband. Then you are to breathe out all of the bad energy he has sent to you. Jaguar transforms things, and the rattle breaks up energy patterns." She began to drum.

That was my cue to start. I loved how she never asked if I was ready to do something. I wondered what I would have said if she'd asked.

For the first few seconds, my brain wanted to ask questions. *How exactly am I supposed to walk like a jaguar? This is going to look really silly. And I'm shaking the rattle at the same time? That will look really good!* Then my thoughts changed. *I don't care. I want my power back!*

Without further thinking, I picked up the rattle, closed my eyes and imagined myself in a black panther's body. My legs began to move. My hand shook the rattle. I noticed I wanted to be on all fours but the rattle in my hand made that rather challenging. I doubted that I looked anything like a black panther, but I kept my focus on breathing in all the anger, resentment and bad thoughts I had sent Martin's way and I breathed out anything that he'd sent me.

I kept going with my panther walking, rattle shaking, breathing in and out until it felt like I was done. I opened my eyes and stopped shaking the rattle. I felt a bit light-headed and was hoping that was because I had released and transformed so much energy.

We did a couple more healing processes. I was feeling much lighter inside.

Then Kimberley said, "You are going to begin visualising the spot where you will spend the night, so that each day you can send it energy." I could feel my heart beating as I closed my eyes. That solo-night was getting closer.

> *I imagined myself walking on a path. My view was from above, as if I was looking down at a map, and I saw a beam of light going off to the left. I followed it, and it lead to a big, smooth stone, so smooth it looked like it had been sanded. There was a groove in the middle of it just the right size for my body, as if the stone was the palm of a huge hand. There was a reddish tinge around one edge of the stone, a mountain was on one side and thick bush below. I imagined sending light to the stone and the area.*

I opened my eyes, wondering what the place would really look like when I got there.

After that, we called it a day. "Tomorrow we will start making your prayer ties," she said as I was leaving. These prayer ties would come with me for my night in the desert. While making wishes and prayers for protection and for the good of myself, others and the planet, I would wrap up little bundles of herbs in small square pieces of cloth and attach each one separately to a long piece of string. The intention was that my prayers would be sent out to the heavens and would surround me during the night to keep me safe, which was good, because I needed all the help I could get.

Of the six-day retreat, three of the days were half-days. Kimberley suggested that I use the time on my own to practice my shamanic skills, to listen to my intuition, and to visit some of the sacred sites nearby.

On one of the days, I decided to climb one of the big, alluring red rocks. I had noticed this rock when Kimberley was introducing me to the area and had felt a strong pull to go to it then, but we didn't have time. I loved the shape of it, similar to a bell. It was called Bell Rock.

My whole body felt energised as I walked there. I looked down at the ground. *There is something about this red earth, maybe it's just the colour or maybe something else that really excites me.* My attention moved to my very comfy grey sneakers, and I smiled feeling grateful for them yet again.

As I walked along the trail I thought, *I don't want to be just a tourist on a hike. I want to make this a meaningful adventure.*

I decided to create two intentions for my walk. The intention I thought of right away was an expansion of the first shamanic journey I had taken to "remember who I am," because I wanted to keep opening myself to that reality. My second intention was to find a walking stick. I had a vision of having one with me on my solo-night.

A few other travellers were coming towards me on the narrowing path just before the big climb. Stepping aside to let them pass, I noticed the woman held in her hand a big stick. It looked hand-carved. "That's a marvellous walking stick you have," I said to her. She smiled and held it out to me. "Do you want it? I'm flying back to Germany tomorrow and can't take it with me."

Really!? How magical is that? Holding my new walking stick with astonishment, I continued on my way. Knowing I would soon need both hands to climb, I tucked my stick behind a distinctively-gnarled, fallen, Juniper tree. *I'll pick it up on the way back.*

As I continued my ascent, I paid attention to where I felt drawn to climb. I soon strayed off the designated trail to climb higher. Needing my whole body to climb, I pulled myself up over ledges and steep reaches. I felt exhilarated and fearless. I had no thoughts fearing I might get lost or that it might be too dangerous. I climbed higher and higher.

It was so freeing to climb. I could go wherever I wanted. It didn't matter if I got to the top or not. I just wanted to climb and go as I high as I could.

Finally, I stood on the highest ledge I could reach and lay down laughing from the rapture of the climb. The warmth of the red rock on my back was soothing, and the warmer rays of sun brushed softly over the front of my body with a gentle wind. What an astounding journey I had been on so far.

I recalled that question Rebecca had asked me in the café, in what seemed like another lifetime, "What would you do if time and money were not an issue?"

"I would do it all!" was my reply, and here I was doing it all.

I looked up into the sky and noticed a few dark clouds gathering. Rain would be coming soon and it was time to head back down.

I bum slid down the first ledge and looked for the next step. Nothing appeared obvious. I walked along the ledge searching, but I could not find a step down. I checked along the ledge again, this time more slowly. Nothing.

A chill ran down my neck. I was so high and so far away from the trail. *If I get stuck up here, no one will find me for days. Maybe it wasn't such a good idea to have wandered so far off the trail.*

"Relax. Slow down," I whispered.

Looking up, I saw a bird in the sky. This was the perfect time to use the nature work I had been practicing. I held the question in my mind. *How do I get down?* I watched the bird.

It swooped to the right, indicating for me to go to the right.

"But I just came from that way," I mumbled as I went to the right anyway.

I heard a voice speak. "Sometimes you have to

back to go forward". It was the voice of the rock. I was surrounded by wisdom. Sure enough, I found the next step down. But then I was stuck yet again.

Then it dawned on me. My head was trying to find a solution, but I hadn't climbed with my head. I had climbed with my body. If my body got me up, my body could get me down. I felt something shift inside as I registered this—a resolute focus that my body was going to get me down the rock.

I spoke out loud. "Head, you are off-line. Body, it's all yours. Get me down."

Without any further thought, my body moved. It moved fast, instinctually and without pause. I felt like a wild cat, a black panther, in fact, gracefully manoeuvring the ledges. Within moments, I was back at the bottom of the rock and on the marked trail.

Taking in a long, deep breath, I sighed a hugely grateful, "Thank you." I looked back in the direction I had come from. I couldn't see any path. It was just steep rock face. My heart was thumping in my chest, but this time with excitement and joy at what had just happened.

My attention moved to more earthly things, like retrieving my stick. I saw the gnarled, fallen Juniper and looked behind it, but the stick wasn't there. My heart sunk. *Someone has found my treasure, and now I have lost it.* Then I had a second thought. *What if this is the wrong tree?*

Looking around, I saw another old dead tree with twisted bark. Filled with hope, I looked behind it, but again no stick. Then I noticed something I hadn't seen before, something that made my heart really feel heavy. There weren't just one or two old dead trees with twisted bark, there were hundreds. And there wasn't just one marked trail going up the rock, there were at least half a dozen and they all looked the same, marked with posts and rope. *I think I followed this trail, or maybe that trail over there.* I hadn't paid attention to the trail I took assuming it was the only one. My stick was surely behind one of those trees along one of those trails, but which one?

I let out a big breath. *It's only a stick. I can walk away from it. I can find another.*

On the verge of giving up, I thought of something else. I remembered how I got down the rock. Once again, my head could not figure this out. My body knew where the stick was.

I quietened my mind, and holding the image of the stick, I asked my body to find it. My breathing slowed down. My eyes softened as I paid attention to where my body felt inclined to walk. As I moved in a particular direction, I could hear commentary from my head saying things like, *It can't be over there. I didn't even walk that way.* I ignored these thoughts and kept following where I felt drawn to go.

Within a few minutes, I found my stick.

That night in bed, I wondered if the day's events were two of the four transformative incidents foretold by the dragonfly, or if they were the warning I needed to pay attention to. It was comforting to think that maybe I had already been warned and understood the warning, but something deep inside told me it was still yet to come.

Chapter 24

I sat outside in the quiet, still-dark morning, my hands wrapped around a mug of hot water and lemon. The day had finally arrived when I would go into the desert and stay the night alone. The plan was to stay awake all night and witness nature from sunset to sunrise at the same time as I witnessed my own inner journey through fear.

I felt unshakably calm, despite the fact that I was about to spend the night out in the open with any number of wild beings. It was only morning, but then I had spent a whole week preparing for this day with meditations, visualisations and prayers.

Some movement on the ground got my attention. In the dim light, a greyish coloured toad, the size of a big fist, hopped right in front of me, about one metre away. We looked at each for a while. He didn't move. I didn't move. *Maybe he's a pet and wants some food.* I wondered what toads eat as I searched in my memory for what food I had in my fridge.

But what's a toad doing in the desert? Don't they need water? Looking at the toad, I asked telepathically, "Where do you live?" A picture of a hole in a tree came to my mind, and I assumed this was its response to my question. I didn't really know where toads lived but I certainly wouldn't have thought they lived in trees. An Internet search later that day confirmed that some of them do.

The toad sat staring at me for about five more minutes, then it hopped away. I felt honoured to have had such a visit. Later when I told Kimberley, she smiled and said it was a sign of good fortune. I took in a deep breath. Even though I had prepared so much for my night in the desert, a good luck sign from nature was very welcome.

All too soon it was after dinner. I packed my bag. I was starting to feel nervous, and my fingers shook a little as I put each item in my knapsack: a couple of merino tops, a jacket, my thick woollen shawl, a water bottle, my camera, my prayer ties, a small piece of tarpaulin, a folded chair, my walking stick, and a flashlight. That was all I was allowed to take.

Holding the flashlight, I recalled an evening when I had asked Kimberley, "What if a wild animal comes along? How do I defend myself?"

She took a deep breath, expanded her chest, stood on her tiptoes, her arms out from her sides, and said, "Make yourself really big and flicker your flashlight in their eyes. And don't step out of your medicine wheel!"

I put the flashlight in my bag.

It was time to go.

Kimberley dropped me off at the desert canyon entrance and said, "I'll come for you at dawn. When you hear my drum, blow this whistle. Then I'll know you've heard me. I'll wait fifteen minutes. If you don't come out in that time, I will come in to get you." With that, she rolled up her window and drove away.

Her words were not very reassuring, but what else

could she have said? "Enjoy your evening"? "Have a good time"? "Good luck"?

All of my attention was devoured by the sound of her tires on the dirt road as she turned around and headed out. I held my gaze on the canyon and away from her four-wheel drive for fear I might end up running after her in terror shouting, "Don't leave me here by myself!"

I clenched my fists to hold myself back from doing just that.

When I could no longer hear her vehicle, I made my way to the canyon entrance track. At least that's what Kimberley called it. Really it was a nondescript, unmarked pathway that could have easily been missed. The sun was low in the horizon and I would have about an hour before sunset.

Taking a deep breath, I entered.

I had never been a confident hiker or camper. As much as I loved the bush, I usually stayed on marked pathways—apart from my daring climb up Bell Rock—or I went with someone who knew the way. This was the first time I had entered unknown bush, on a completely unmarked trail, on my own. I squeezed my walking stick, as if I was squeezing someone's hand to reassure myself.

Kimberley said the rangers didn't allow overnight campers, so if I got caught it would be better not to have a tent. "Stay out in the open and keep yourself out of sight of the road," she said. "Don't go near any bushes, trees or caves. Other beings go there to sleep." Staying out in the open was the last thing I wanted to do, but I was going to follow everything she had told me.

I paused for a moment and closed my eyes. I wanted to follow the trail that I had seen in my vision. It was still clear in my mind. A white light went off on a trail to the left. I opened my eyes and kept walking, looking for the trail to the left, and before long, I found it.

All of my senses were alert as I walked slowly paying attention to the trees, the bushes, the rocks, and the ground. I had never walked with a walking stick before and it felt awkward in my hands. The weight of my knapsack pressed down on my back and I was glad I wasn't going for a long hike. Kimberley had said not to go too far in.

I was looking for my spot—the place where I would set myself up for my night vigil.

I came across a flat piece of rock. *This must be it.* I walked around the area, listening to my body. Something didn't quite feel right, so I decided to keep going.

I stepped up onto a smooth piece of flat rock overlooking the valley. Something about it felt familiar. My eyes studied the rock. It had an indent in the middle big enough to hold me, and there was a light reddish tinge on one side. My heart began to beat with excitement. *Could this be what I saw in my visualisations?*

I looked up. There was a cliff face to one side, like a mountain, and there were bushes below in the valley. Tears filled my eyes. This was exactly what I had seen in my visions. I was overwhelmed with awe and gratitude that I had trusted my vision and listened to the forces guiding me through the unfamiliar canyon to this spot.

With little time to spare before dark, I set about my

first task: creating the medicine wheel I would stay inside of all night. The medicine wheel was traditionally used by Native American tribes as a tool for insight and healing. As I stood in the spot where I planned to make mine, I remembered Kimberley saying, "Stay inside your medicine wheel. It is where you have been sending all of the energy. It is your power spot."

I watched my trembling hands pick up four big rocks and feel their weight, their rough and smooth edges, as I placed them in the four directions: north, east, south and west.

Adding smaller rocks in between holding down my prayer ties, I imagined myself being confronted by some wild beast and using my stick and my flashlight to shoo them away. It was funny for a second, and then it wasn't. Suddenly I felt painfully vulnerable. The tension was rising in me, and full-blown fear was about to run wild. I had to interrupt the process, and quickly. My conversation with myself went like this:

"What if a mountain li……"

"Nope."

"But what if….."

"Nope."

"But….."

"Nope."

I turned my attention to unpacking the tarpaulin and putting on warmer clothes in preparation for the night, and my mind became still again.

Sitting in the middle of my medicine wheel, I watched

the most glorious sunset I had ever seen: pink, red, blue, grey, black. As the sun disappeared, the grey and black took over the sky. Then all of a sudden I saw a flash of lightening. Then thunder. Then a drop of water landed on my head. Then two. Within seconds, I was in the middle of a raging thunderstorm. The cosy spot in the smooth rock where I had nestled was now turning into a puddle.

For a moment I thought of moving to higher ground, but I remembered that I was not to step outside of the circle. I shuffled my body over to the one side of my wheel, where the rock was slightly higher.

Darn. I was looking forward to relaxing, and here I am fighting with the elements.

Pointlessly, I clutched the sides of the skimpy square piece of tarpaulin and sat there shivering, wishing the storm would pass. Then I remembered: this is my journey. The worst thing that could happen was that I would get very wet. *Big deal.* My body relaxed, and I relaxed into the puddle, surrendering to the sensation of water seeping into the back of my clothing.

After about two hours, the rain subsided and the clouds cleared. I poked my head out from the tarpaulin and stared up at the sky. The stars twinkled. The familiar and soothing sound of crickets chirping surrounded me. There must have been thousands of them out there in the desert night, and they sang as if they were one big cricket, starting on the same note and stopping at the same time. *How do they know when to start and when to stop?*

I reflected on my relationship with Martin. Was this the same knowing when to start and when to stop? In one of my meditations during the final two months on the farm, I had asked why he and I got married in the first place if we were only going to separate.

> *I saw a vision of us both walking on a path together. It felt good. Then a second path appeared off to the right. We stood where the paths were parting, and with all the love in my heart I said to him, "This is the point where I go this way, my dear," as I pointed to the other path.*

When I opened my eyes from that meditation, there were tears streaming down my cheeks. My heart was aching with grief, and yet at the same time, it felt so right. *Is it really that simple? Had our relationship simply come to its natural conclusion? And did that mean there was no one to blame?*

Suddenly, a branch snapped in the valley below. Adrenaline shot through my veins. I held my breath, alert to every sound. There was a wild animal nearby, and it was big enough to break a branch. Was it a pig? A coyote? A deer? A mountain lion? I stayed very still as the terror rose within me. I knew it would smell my fear.

"Don't let fear get you," Kimberley had said during one of our sessions. "Look up into the stars and let it go."

I looked up into the sky and focused all my attention on the stars as if my life depended on it. My breath came back. My heart slowed down.

More and more stars appeared. There were red ones, blue ones, green ones, gold ones. They sparkled like crystals. Some of them disappeared and then came back. A shooting star flew across the sky. *One*, I counted in my mind. I held my hand up in front of my face, but I couldn't see it. The blackness consumed me.

Two. As I lay completely still looking into the depths of the sky, I stopped feeling my body. The feeling of separateness left me, and I began to merge with the black sky. I was consciousness witnessing the stars. As I breathed, the sky breathed. My mind wandered in and out of this vast state of consciousness.

Three. Sleep was calling me, but I kept a vigilant watch over the sky and the shooting stars.

Four. What time is it? I didn't really want to know. I had purposely left my watch behind so I wouldn't be thinking about the time.

Five. Five shooting stars!

When the dawn began to lift the heavy blanket of black, there was something relieving about the coming of light and the return of my sight. I sat up and watched the dark forms around me appear in the shapes of bushes, trees and rocks. A few noisy bats flew by my head, making their way back to their nests after their night out.

I watched the horizon, until the golden light made its first peek into the day. I had made it from sunset to sunrise.

Then I heard the drum. *So soon.* I didn't want to leave just yet. I wanted to watch the whole sunrise.

I blew the whistle in response and quickly packed up. Putting my things in my bag I was feeling a bit smug. *That was easy. Apart from that one little fright in the night. I made it!* I was feeling pretty triumphant, having faced a couple of big fears, such as walking into unknown bush with no marked trail; and staying out all night in the desert along with all the wildlife. Now my adventure was over, and I could relax.

I entered the bush to head back onto the path, but I came to a dead-end. The bush was too thick to pass through. *I'm sure I came out of the bush at this point.* I stepped back and tried entering at another point. Dead-end. I continued to look for openings, but each one led to an impasse.

I knew I came through an opening in the bush, but I couldn't find it. The storm had washed away any signs of the track I had taken.

Fifteen minutes would soon be up. "I have to get out of here!" I shouted in alarm at the bushes, as if they were intentionally standing in my way.

Panic was starting to take over. A part of me, the part that observes everything with a calm, objective eye, found this situation amusing and was sure that there was some deep and meaningful parallel with my life—a lesson to be learned—but the rest of me didn't find it funny at all.

Kimberley's drum beat again. *Fifteen minutes must be up! I can't let her come in to get me! This can't end with me being rescued!*

A small, quiet voice inside me said, "Relax, Leanne." But it was too late. In a wild panic, I started to cry and ran aimlessly into the bush, bashing into bushes and trees, and dropping my stick.

Where are you going? What are you doing? I imagined my inner critic standing there with a clipboard, shaking her head and making notes. "Failing to stay calm. Fell apart in the last test."

"STOP!" another voice inside me yelled. I paused, panting. "What are you doing?" the voice said, taking charge. "You know what to do. The mountains are on the left, and the tree-covered hills are on the right. Walk in between them!"

The strong, directive voice overrode my panic, and I followed its instructions, knowing I would find my way. My breathing returned to normal as I pushed through the thick bush and squeezed between the trees. "Go this way," the voice said, and a vision of a small tree flashed in my mind. I recognised that tree as one I had just passed. I looked behind me, and there it was. I went back and climbed up a small path beside the tree, and there was the trail I was looking for.

I wiped the sweat from my forehead and exhaled a long, deep breath. *I found it.* But as I walked on the familiar dirt trail back to the road where Kimberley was waiting, my feelings of accomplishment were mixed with disappointment. *How could you let yourself get so upset? How many times does it take for you to tell yourself to stop and slow…?*

Almost immediately, other thoughts drowned out the critical inner voice.

So I panicked. So what? I just spent the whole night on my own in the desert, faced some fears—and now just faced my worst fear: being lost—but I listened to my intuition and found my way. How amazing is that?

A real feeling of victory took over. *How much courage did it take to face all of that?*

Taking in a full breath, feeling deeply satisfied, I said aloud to the trees, "I made it."

Kimberley had just set out on the path to meet me when I came out of the canyon entrance. "Welcome back," she said with a big, embracing smile.

Back at her house, blueberry pancakes with maple syrup were the perfect way to complete my adventure. Over breakfast, we debriefed my journey.

Kimberley reinforced that I was being reminded to listen to my intuition and follow my instincts. Then she asked, "What was your lesson in finding your way back?"

I reflected for a moment. The message was obvious: that it was time for me to create a new path and to stop looking for the old one. I shared that with Kimberley and she nodded. I didn't know exactly what this meant for my life, but I trusted that its meaning would become clear in time.

As the last moments of my shamanic journey with Kimberley came to an end, I savoured a mouthful of pancake and recalled the dragonfly's message foretelling a warning. I knew it was referring to my night in the desert, and I had no doubt that had I not paid vigilant attention to all of Kimberley's instructions, my night would have been very different.

The other events—getting stuck up the rock and coming down, finding my stick, following my intuition to find the place I had envisioned for my medicine wheel and finding my way back from my vision quest—had all served to open my awareness of who I was and what I was capable of. Those, I guessed, were the four transformative events that the dragonfly foretold.

I felt like a whole lifetime had passed during my week in Sedona.

I turned my attention back to Kimberley, and to my breakfast, taking the time to fully appreciate the moment. When I had finished my last pancake, I used my finger to clean the plate. No maple syrup should ever go to waste.

I could feel sleep calling me after the deficit of the night before and was grateful I'd had the foresight to book two more days in the bedsit to do nothing after so much adventure. To assist in my relaxation, I had booked in with a highly-recommended masseur. After everything I'd been through, I was looking forward to totally blissing out.

Chapter 25

Daniel came with his massage table under his arm and greeted me with gentle blue eyes and a warm smile. He was the same height as me, one-point-seven metres, with an average but strong build. I knew immediately I would be in good hands. While he set things up in my room, we chatted away as if we were best friends who hadn't seen each other in years.

"We'd better start the massage," he said after half an hour had glided by.

He worked diligently and skilfully. His hands found all of the right spots, and I had no resistance to his touch as I surrendered the tension that had been accumulating in my body for months. Years.

The wafting scents of rose and lavender essential oils were intoxicating, and soon my thoughts began to stray as I fantasised about what a wonderful lover he must be, knowing where to touch and how much pressure to apply. I hadn't had thoughts like that since meeting Aaron on the flight to London.

"I'll leave you to get dressed," he said quietly before he left the room.

Oh darn. It's over. My body could barely move it was so relaxed.

I managed to get dressed and staggered out into the courtyard. Daniel was sitting in one of the chairs waiting for me. "You need a cup of tea," he said decidedly as he helped himself to my supplies in the kitchenette. I nodded, sinking into the other chair and making no effort to help him find anything.

Again the conversation flowed easily. We could have talked all day. After what must have been more than an hour, he said, "I have to get to my yoga class," and he gathered up the last of his things. Four hours had slipped by already.

We felt so familiar and relaxed with each other that instead of shaking hands, we hugged each other goodbye. My whole body leaned up against his. Neither of us moved. My nose took in his scent. A pleasant, woody smell. Nice.

Our legs, hips, bellies, chests and shoulders were touching, unmoving. *How long should a hug last? There is a maximum length of time that a friendly hug can last before one of you pulls away*. It wasn't like there were rules, but there was a boundary one didn't go beyond with a friend. We were definitely passing that boundary.

We still didn't move. My body began to tingle and to come alive in a way it hadn't in years. I thought I had lost my ability to feel sensual, but to my joy, it was still very much there. I felt as if I was sinking into him. His lips touched my neck, and I leaned in closer, opening up my neck to him. Our lips found each other's, and within moments we were tearing our clothes off. Skin touching skin.

Hallelujah! I thanked all the divine beings I could think of as my body remembered, after such a long fast, the joy of making love. Afterwards, we lay in bed, his arms cradling me, chatting about deep and meaningful things just as we had done when we first met.

I told him about the cabin in the woods that I had reserved, and I invited him to join me there. I didn't even know him, and there I was inviting him to come to an isolated cabin with me. *How reckless. How bold. How carefree. How exciting!*

He looked at me very calmly and tenderly. "Call me when you come back from the Canyon, and if you still want me to join you, I will." I was leaving for the Grand Canyon the next day for three days and then returning to Sedona to spend four days in the little cabin. *How wise of him.* Who knew what would change between now and then.

My heart did a little jig while the rest of me smiled a big smile, but then I had a second thought. *What if, really, he doesn't want to come but doesn't want to hurt my feelings by saying no?* My smile faded, but only slightly. *If we are meant to see each other again, we will.* And in any case, any further time with Daniel would have to wait, because I had a date with the Grand Canyon.

I gripped the rail, trying to grapple with the canyon's vastness. It was deeper than I had ever imagined, wider than I could even see. Red, brown and grey layers of rock had been etched out over eons by the flow of the Colorado River.

As I looked down into the canyon, my chest expanded, and the physical sense of my body disappeared. It wasn't called "Grand" for nothing.

I found a path descending into the canyon and followed it. The ranger said it was a three hour hike to the bottom, but a one-day return trip wasn't recommended because of the intense midday heat. Not wanting to put myself in danger, I decided to go as far as I could and then come back up in a total of three hours.

My feet were steady on the well-trodden broken stone path. As I walked, my thoughts drifted to Daniel. I wondered if I should text him. *Just to let him know I'm thinking about him. But maybe that will be too much. He might feel like I'm coming on too strong. But what if he thinks I'm not interested?*

I noticed that I no longer felt present and free inside. I was too busy thinking about how to get what I wanted. Pausing for a moment, I gazed at the rock edges of the canyon, carved by the continual flow of the river. As much as I wanted to think that I had surrendered to the flow of my life, my habit when faced with change was actually to hold on more tightly and try as much as possible to influence the outcome. This had only led to pain.

When I was leaving Martin, much of the suffering I felt was caused by holding on to my expectations of how I thought Martin should be and expectations of how I thought we should separate. Now here I was with Daniel, fearing he might not want to spend time with me and having thoughts about what I should do to get things to go the way I wanted them to rather than just giving in to the natural flow.

Along the path was a big flat rock, and I felt drawn to lie on it. I lay on my belly, very still, and closed my eyes. A question came to my mind, so I asked the rock,

"How do I let go of thinking and analysing and trying to control things so much?"

The rock then took me on a little journey.

> *I began to feel the sensation of the rock moving and sliding down into the canyon. My body reacted quickly. My muscles constricted as I gripped the rock. I would have leaped off it, but my conscious mind knew the rock wasn't really slipping. It was showing me my habit of resisting the flow whenever the flow seems to be going somewhere I didn't want to go.*

If the rock really is falling into the canyon and this is my time, then why resist?

I was aware of the courage it would take to stop resisting and let go. I felt altered inside from my interaction with the rock, as if something inside me had begun to give way to the flow of the river of life.

I decided to not text Daniel.

Continuing to step down the rocky cavern path, I held the same question in my mind: "How do I let go of thinking and analysing and trying to control things so much?" I wanted to ask Eagle for some insight. My mind recalled the time I walked like Jaguar. I wondered if I walked like Eagle, would I access Eagle wisdom?

I looked around to see if anyone was coming, because I knew that what I was about to do was going to look pretty darn silly. No one was around. I closed my eyes for a moment, and in my mind I saw a big, splendid eagle. I envisioned myself inside of the eagle's body and imagined it walking. I opened my eyes. My legs crouched a bit as I began to walk. My arms came out by my sides as if they were wings flapping, and I held the vision of the bird in my mind as I walked like Eagle.

Then an extraordinary thing happened. Within moments, I saw an actual eagle, then another one, and then three more. Five real eagles flew above me in the sky. *You're kidding? Are they responding to my call? Really?* There were many eagles in the canyon, and it was possible that they would have been there anyway. *It doesn't matter. I don't need to know.*

Watching the graceful birds I put my question to them. I heard a word in my head in response, "Watch." It was as if they were inviting me to keep my attention on them. Then one of the birds tipped its head up and started to fly almost upside down, following its head. At first I thought maybe it was unwell and was having a seizure of some kind, but then I noticed it was flying fine and steady and it had just done a complete back flip.

Did I really see that? My mouth hung open as I kept staring at the bird. Then it dove into the eagle beside it. *Was it attacking the other bird? Maybe it was dizzy from the back flip?* I was stunned as the two birds seemed to innocently frolic in the sky. Then they stopped frolicking and the five of them flew off together.

Looking down at my feet and the ground I took note: black strapped hiking sandals, rock and dirt path under me. Yes, I was still standing firmly on the ground. This hadn't been a daydream or a visualisation. I had just witnessed an unbelievable display of nature. And this was their answer to my question.

I pondered the meaning of what I had seen as I continued my descent into the Canyon, doing the Leanne walk now.

If I were to do a back flip, that is if I could, I would not be able to do it by trying to analyse what each limb is supposed to do and to then control every muscle to perform the act. I would have to let go and allow my body to do it. But my body couldn't do it by itself. Clear intention and effort would be needed. It would be a dance between holding conscious intention, focused effort and letting go.

What a profound message. This, in a way, was what I had been practicing during my whole journey: in Glastonbury, Malta, New York, with my luggage, the week in Sedona, even leaving Martin. The struggle for me now was bringing this skill into the area of relationships. Rather than practicing *conscious intention, focused effort and holding on,* my lesson was to practice *conscious intention, focused effort and letting go.*

That night, I set my alarm clock for three in the morning. On my way out of the Canyon the day before, I had spotted the perfect viewing place for sunrise: a big flat ledge giving a full view of the horizon.

Arriving in the grey-black before dawn, I saw that I was not the only one who'd had this idea. There were five of us gathered there. No one spoke. We didn't even acknowledge each other. There was something comforting about being there together in silence, sharing a sacred moment, each in our own personal space.

I pulled the woollen shawl closer around my neck as my eyes explored the horizon. Black outlines of trees and rock formations of the canyon began to take shape around me against the background of the dim glow of a sun still shadowed by the earth. As the darkness receded, colour began to take its place. Then came the peak moment. My thinking mind hushed. All my attention moved to where the earth and sky met.

A tiny ridge of liquid gold appeared on the horizon. It was like watching a birth as the sun gradually revealed its whole, glorious self. I too was birthing into a new life, a new life of courage to be my glorious self. What a perfect way to leave this place.

Driving back to Sedona, I felt at peace regarding Daniel. I would be happy to see him and I would be just as happy to spend the next few days on my own. A phone call would reveal all.

Chapter 26

Putting on my sun hat, I leaned back in the chair on the deck of my little wooden cabin—tucked away in the trees—and put my feet up on the railing. This would be my haven for the next four days. Below, the creek happily gurgled along, and the afternoon sun deliciously soothed and warmed my skin. I sighed the most heavenly sigh.

Just to add to the ecstasy, Daniel was coming to join me for the last two days.

Glorious meditation time with precious alone space for reflection, a beautiful, nurturing environment, and my own private masseur and lover. What more could a girl ask for?

My days at the cabin were filled with walks along the creek, naked swims in the deep water holes, yoga on the grass, writing, meditating, eating delicious, fresh, homemade food and making love.

Even though Daniel was with me for only two days, we had fallen into a lovely rhythm of preparing meals together and sharing about important things like relationships, our childhoods and spiritual experiences. I wanted it to continue forever, but too soon, the final day came.

I packed up the last of my things and did a final check through the cabin to make sure I hadn't left anything behind. "Don't forget your towel," Daniel called out from the kitchen, where he was making some lunch for me to take on my four-hour drive to Tucson to attend the spiritual conference.

"Thank you, sweetie," I said, peeking my head around the corner to watch him. *He is so thoughtful and caring.* My heart warmed just looking at him.

I sighed and knew I was going to miss him. I had loved every moment of our time together. Deep down, I knew this was all it would ever be and all it was meant to be, but that didn't stop my heart from hurting and wanting more.

Looking into his caring, clear blue eyes as he handed me my lunch, my tears began to flow. He wrapped his arms around me and rocked me gently, whispering, "You're going to be okay."

I knew I was going to be okay, but for a brief, insecure moment I wanted him to say, "Don't leave. Stay with me." In that desperate moment, driven by childhood fears of not being loved or wanted, I fantasised giving up everything and changing all my plans just to hold on to him a little bit longer.

It took courage to pull myself away from my yearnings and fears to come back into the depths of my heart, where I knew the truth. Deep inside my heart, I was glad he didn't ask me to stay, because I wouldn't have. I didn't want to. The feeling of peace in this deep place was unwavering. I had let go.

Daniel didn't have to leave so early, so he stayed behind to close up the cabin. As I climbed into the car tenderly holding my lunch, he stood there watching.

"Drive safely," he said, waving to me as I pulled out of the driveway. I nodded—which was all I could manage with my eyes blurred from tears—and tried to focus on keeping to the right-hand side of the road.

I knew I would never see him again.

PART 3

Open Me to freedom

"Hold the vision. Let go
of the plan."

Chapter 27

After I had driven for a couple of hours, the tears dried and I felt calmer, but I was still grateful that the road to Tucson was straight, so I didn't need to worry about navigation.

I had expected to feel excited about the conference, with the meditations, talks and healing sessions, but by the time I arrived in Tucson I was so emotionally drained, maybe from all of the crying, that it was difficult to feel anything.

The aesthetically pleasing landscaped entrance—with stones, plants and a fountain—to the luxury five-star hotel was a stark contrast to the intimate, rustic setting I had come from. The expansive grounds boasted two eighteen-hole golf courses and three swimming pools, among other facilities. But looking up at the gorgeous chandelier in the middle of the spacious foyer, I felt oddly detached.

This was such a shift from how I had been feeling only four hours earlier. I didn't know what was wrong, but something wasn't right.

There were hundreds of people milling around me as I stood in the middle of the lobby with my suitcase by my side, feeling disoriented. I had been in and stayed at many large hotels, but for some reason I felt lost and unable to identify where the front desk was. People were moving around me in all directions. "Excuse me!" someone said, and I stepped out of their way. *Where am I supposed to go?* I was longing for my little cabin.

Then it got worse. My vision began to close in and I could only see what I was directly looking at. I could feel my consciousness retreating inside becoming more and more separate. It was like I was behind a door and could only peek out at the world through the keyhole. All sound was muffled as if my hands were covering my ears. I could hear people talking but their voices were muddled together into one big murmur.

Somehow I made my way to the front desk. The woman at the desk was asking questions, and I could hear a voice answering, but the voice was strange—like an empty echo in my mind. I was horrified when I realised the voice belonged to me. Words were coming out of my mouth, but I wasn't connected with them. I was not present. There were no feelings at all inside me. I was numb.

I knew I needed help.

I could have told myself I'd had such an emotional time with Daniel that now my heart was closing to protect myself. I could have decided to have a nap and sleep it off, or I could have gone to the bar for a glass of wine to forget about it.

But I didn't do any of those things.

"Are there any very big, old trees close by?" I asked the woman at the desk.

She gave me a curious look. "Not that I know of," she said. "But there is a three-hundred-year-old cactus on the property."

I knew that was where I needed to go.

I found the cactus right next to one of the entrances to the hotel, where the road had been built around him. He was at least ten metres high, with many arms growing out of his ribbed body. He stood audacious and proud, the granddaddy of cacti.

I stood a few metres away so I could see his grandeur. My breath slowed in his presence, and I felt the centre of my chest open as a feeling of love flowed naturally from me to him.

In Sedona, when I was visiting the sacred sites, Kimberley introduced me to a ritual. We were facing one of the big red rocks, and she said, "Send it energy from the centre of your chest. Then ask its permission to be on the land." When I did this, I could feel energy come back to me from the rock.

Facing the cactus now, I felt love flow back to me.

In my mind I held the question, "Do I have your blessing to be on this land?"

A very deep and powerfully rich male voice sounded clearly in my mind, "Yes, Little One."

I stayed there until sunset, feeling a constant flow of soothing, healing energy from his trunk to the core of my body. I was completely in love with him. I decided I would meditate with him each morning.

Feeling grounded and at peace in myself once again, I wandered back into the hotel.

Within thirty minutes, I had made several new friends. We were all attending the same conference, and as we happily huddled together in the lobby's big lounge chairs sharing our stories, I completely forgot about my earlier feelings of disorientation.

I felt present and connected.

One woman in particular intrigued me. Edith was a tiny woman whose crippling rheumatoid arthritis was the least of the obstacles she had faced to get to this conference. "I have all of Eckhart Tolle's books," she said. "And Louise Hay's, Esther Hicks', Wayne Dyer's. I could go on." Her eyes sparkled as she spoke. "You would love my bookshelf. Every time I hear about a new spiritual book that inspires me, I take some money from the petty cash, and I go and buy it. I've read them all, and I've heard about the courses they run and the conferences. I dreamed about going, but I knew I never would..." Her voice trailed off.

"Why?" I asked, assuming it was because of her arthritis.

"I can't leave my husband, my children and my grandchildren. It would mean taking time away from them to do something for myself. How selfish!"

I sensed anger inside of her.

"Why are you here then?" I asked interested to know what happened to change things.

She smiled. "My husband insisted. He told me I had to go because he had already paid for it." She squeezed my hand. "I am so excited! I never imagined that I would do something like this."

I thought about the physical pain I experienced at the end of my marriage and how when I released my emotions, through writing those therapeutic letters to Martin and to myself, the pain had disappeared. I couldn't help but wonder if Edith's emotional situation had in any way contributed to her arthritis.

The morning was chilly, but interestingly I wasn't feeling the cold. As I brought awareness back into my body, I felt the hard stone underneath me. I wriggled my toes, feeling them tucked underneath my knees. When I opened my eyes, I saw the cactus in front of me. I had felt warm and protected meditating in his presence.

I stood up and stretched my arms out as the sun peeked over the hills. *Another glorious day in Arizona.*

It was the second day of the conference, and it was also my birthday—my real birthday. I had decided that my gift to myself was a full day to go wherever I felt guided to be. Carrying my notebook and a mug of black coffee, I headed to the conference hall for the morning session. Not feeling drawn to go inside, I paused. A palo verde tree, native to Arizona, with bushy light green foliage was near the hall and looked inviting, so I steered my steps in its direction.

As I was walking toward the tree, I passed a woman I met on the first evening. "Good morning!" she said. "Aren't you going in?"

"Nope. For my birthday I've decided that I'm going to do whatever I want to do, and right now I want to go and sit under that tree."

She smiled. "I was thinking about taking a little break for myself, too. Mind if I join you?"

Our conversation was easy as we talked about relationships, health and healing, but after some time, my attention began to wander. I wasn't bored, but my attention kept drifting, so I made more effort to listen.

It was nearing break time for the people in the conference, and I felt a pull to sit on a big rock near the entrance to the hall. In the past, I might have ignored this feeling, not wanting to interrupt my new friend while she was sharing about deep, personal things. But I had an agreement with myself, so I said, "I'm really sorry, but I have this strong urge to go and sit on that rock and be there for when the people come outside for their break."

She nodded as if she completely understood. "I'll catch you later," she said with a smile, and she walked back toward the conference hall. *What a lovely person.*

As I sat on the rock feeling the warmth of the sun emanating into my hands, the hall doors opened and people began spilling out. Immediately, a woman who I hadn't met before walked straight up to me and said, "I have a gift for you." *There's no way she could know it's my birthday.* She held out a little bag. "Choose one," she said. I peered into the opened bag. Inside was a collection of stones and crystals. Deciding to let my fingers choose, I closed my eyes and put my hand inside. Feeling around I chose something smooth that wasn't a stone or a crystal and put it into my palm. It was a ring made of shiny black crystal. I looked at her, feeling very grateful. "Thank you. You didn't know it's my birthday today."

"Well, isn't this perfect then? Happy birthday!" She looked down at my hand. "Ah, black onyx. Good for protection and feeling grounded." Our eyes gazed into each other's for a few seconds and then she wandered on.

I had no desire to move, so I stayed on the rock.

"Excuse me." I turned to find a man I didn't know standing next to me. There were so many people at the conference, and I had only met a few. "I've opened up a portal for you," he said matter-of-factly. "I don't usually let people know when I've done that, but I wanted to let you know. It's near Sirius."

I looked into his eyes without saying anything. To be honest, I didn't have a clue what he was talking about, but I did appreciate the gift, even if I didn't understand it. I thanked him and he disappeared back into the crowd.

I was still a bit dazed from this interaction when three women walked past me. Suddenly one of them turned and pointed at me. With a big smile, she said, "You're the one who meditates with the cactus! I've seen you in the mornings." I nodded and smiled. "I recognise you," she said. "You are one of the ancient ones."

I sensed that she was honouring me in some way, but I didn't know what to say, so I just smiled, and she carried on her way with her friends.

By this point I was feeling uncomfortably conspicuous. My hands pushed down on the warm rock as I prepared to stand up, but my body didn't want to move, so I stayed put.

My eyes scanned the crowd. People had spread out in small groups under trees, on the grass or on the steps. I spotted Edith—the woman with arthritis who I had met on the first evening—making her way towards me. I smiled, happy to see her again, but her face was drawn and tense. "Leanne, I have to leave." Her voice was full of desperation. She began to cry, and I put my arms around her.

She had a bladder infection. "I get them all the time," she said. "They spread quickly to my kidneys and I almost always have to go to the hospital and get it treated right away. I have to go and I'm so upset." She bit her lip and looked down at her knobby fingers. "My husband used all of our vacation money for me to come here."

"Edith, I have something for you." Sometimes I got bladder infections myself when I was travelling, so I had a small first aid kit filled with remedies for it. I hadn't needed any of them on this trip.

This was what I had been waiting for. It was time to leave the rock.

I gave all my remedies to Edith and asked her if she would like some healing work as well. "That would be wonderful," she said. I asked her to close her eyes. Her aura was very dim and barely visible. I sensed the dimness was indication of her suffering. I closed my eyes and called in my angels, asking them to help me help her.

I visualised a bright light shining into the top of my head and down into my heart. I imagined flowing this powerful light out from my chest into the centre of Edith's chest. I guided her to call in her angels and ask them to help her heal her bladder. I extended my hand above her belly and held the intention that all unhelpful energy infecting her bladder rise into my hand, as if my hand was a magnet. My palm felt hot, dense sensations. In my mind I saw black forms, similar to the shape of clouds, coming out of her body and into my hand. I then asked the angels to clear away all energy that was not mine. I imagined seeing a bright light shining from the centre of Edith's being and flowing light into her bladder.

I opened my eyes and looked at her aura again. The light was brighter and I could see it around her whole head and her shoulders. I knew she was in a better state inside of herself now.

Later that day, I saw Edith again. The colour had returned to her face, and she was animatedly talking with someone during a break. At the end of the day, she came to find me. Reaching for my hands, she said, "Leanne, I feel so much better. The infection is almost gone and I don't have to go to the hospital!" She thanked and hugged me. It was the best birthday gift I could have received.

As the sun lowered in the hills behind the hotel, I looked to the bright red sky and breathed in the warm air. My time in Arizona was coming to an end, and my travels were almost over. I wasn't in a hurry to leave, but I also didn't wish to stay any longer. The timing was just right.

Walking into the hotel my thoughts moved ahead to the final part of my travels. I would be spending the next two weeks in Canada with my Mom before heading home to New Zealand. My excitement to see her and talk about my adventures was mixed with apprehension. Visits with my Mom had always been challenging for me. Regardless of how much personal development work I had done, each time I visited her, I would helplessly regress to the angry teenager I used to be.

I promised myself that this time I was going to be different.

Chapter 28

The sound of my suitcase rolling along the marble floor echoed in the hotel lobby. I was the only person awake at such an early hour, and as I hauled my bag toward my rental car, I said a silent thank you to whoever invented luggage with wheels.

I smiled, remembering the night before, when twenty others from the conference gathered to celebrate my birthday. Someone had organised a surprise birthday cake and a few musicians to serenade us, and at the end of the evening we said our goodbyes and exchanged contact information and hopes that we would meet again someday.

But I still had to say one more goodbye.

Once my bags were in the car, I went back to the hotel entrance. Facing my cactus friend, I whispered, "Goodbye," and tears rolled down my cheeks. My heart was so open.

I could have stayed there all day, but an inner pull tugged me. I glanced at my watch. Six o'clock. Time to go.

When I arrived at the gate for my flight to Canada via Los Angeles, the big, black hand on the wall clock told me I had a luxurious ten minutes to spare. This moment marked the end of my pilgrimage—well, at least the one I had planned.

I had been confronted with so many tests and offered

so many gifts, now every cell of my being felt alive and present—as if I was a butterfly newly hatched from my chrysalis, drying out my wings—strong and yet vulnerable.

I felt free, free to be myself and trusting I could handle whatever circumstances arose. I thought of my Mom and smiled. I was ready.

My mind flickered back to the farm, a lifetime ago. I closed my eyes. Holding an image of Martin in my heart I said this Hawaiian healing prayer in my mind: *I am sorry. Please forgive me. Thank you. I love you.*

Chapter 29

"Honey, do you want coffee?" my Mom called out from upstairs. *Can't she let me sleep?* I was immediately irritated. Still lying in bed, I pulled the covers over my head as if that was going to help. I knew I wouldn't be able to get back to sleep.

I sat up. "No thanks. I'll come upstairs," I shouted, trying to curb the sharpness in my voice. *Why does she annoy me so much? She only asked if I wanted a coffee. She's excited to see me.* I sighed and bowed my head, feeling guilty. Then I remembered I had made a commitment that this visit was going to be different, which made me feel even worse.

"Here you go, honey," Mom said, passing me a mug of hot coffee. My back stiffened. *I said I didn't want coffee.* I pushed down my anger and tried to seem grateful.

"Thanks, Mom." I said. "But I don't want any coffee."

What is it that bothers me about her? She is just being caring. It doesn't make any logical sense. My memory went back to a time when I was four years old. I woke up late at night and called out for my Mom. No one answered. I got up to discover that both of my parents had gone. I thought they had left us, but actually Mom was visiting with a girlfriend and Dad, having woken from a nap, didn't check to see if Mom was in, and decided to go out for a walk. When they finally came home later that night, Mom was really mad with Dad.

In the meanwhile, being the oldest, I decided I had to take care of my two-year-old brother. I pulled him out of his cot, and we built a fort in the living room with the sofas and blankets to protect us. I remembered thinking that the food in the cupboard would only last for so long, and that I would need to get a job, but I would have to lie about my age, because no one would give a job to a four-year-old.

I made a decision then that I had to take care of myself, because I couldn't rely on anyone else. Was I still holding a grudge against my Mom for that? And was that why I resisted her attempts to take care of me?

As I pondered this, I noticed my body had relaxed.

"Would you like some toast?" she asked.

"Sure, Mom. Thanks," I replied with a smile. A real smile.

To help myself keep my promise to make this a positive visit, I decided to create a mantra: "Mom doesn't need to do anything different, and I will keep my heart open and stay in communication with her instead of silently stewing."

I knew this would be a big task, but I was up for the challenge.

The next day, Mom and I decided to go shopping. "Is that all you're going to wear?" Mom asked. *Don't tell me what to wear!*

I repeated my mantra and took a slow, deep breath, bringing my awareness into the centre of my chest.

Instead of ignoring her and going quiet, I looked into her eyes and said, "What else do I need Mom?"

"Well with all that air-conditioning in the malls it's going to be cold. You might want to bring a sweater."

"What a darn good idea." *If I had continued to push her away we would have probably had an argument, I would have felt bad for being so reactive about something so little and it would have affected the rest of our day.*

I breathed a deep sigh of relief. I'd had my first win.

Over the next few days, I had more wins and some losses, but the wins were winning.

I had been keeping in touch with Daniel by email. Even though I knew I would never see him again, I wasn't finished thinking about our tenderness together and his hands on my body. We had arranged that he would call me at one o'clock in the afternoon and I could hardly wait.

"What do you think about that?" Mom asked. She was sitting on the sofa next to me.

"What?" I said shaking my head and realising I hadn't been listening. "Oh sorry, Mom. I'm waiting for this phone call and was thinking about that. Tell me again what you were saying and I'll listen this time."

One o'clock came and passed, but Daniel didn't call. *He's probably really busy. He'll call when he's free.* I continued to try and focus on the conversation with my Mom. The little hand on the clock moved to two. *Maybe we got the time zones wrong and he thought he was supposed to call now.* But he didn't call. Two-thirty. *He did say he would be handling some work things. Maybe something unexpected came up. But if that's the case, why didn't he call to say? Maybe he forgot about me.*

The feeling of being forgotten reminded me of a time when I was thirteen and my Dad didn't show to pick me up from my swimming lesson. He was usually late, so at first I didn't think much of it. He suffered from depression, but we didn't have a name for it then. We just said, "Dad is having a bad day," meaning that he had shut himself away in his room and we shouldn't disturb him.

After fifteen minutes of waiting for Dad to pick me up, I felt annoyed. After twenty-five minutes, I was frightened.

When he pulled up forty minutes later, he could tell by the look on my face I wasn't happy. "I'm sorry honey. I forgot I was picking you up." *How could he forget about me?* I was angry and deeply hurt. *Clearly I'm not very important.* We drove all the way home in silence.

Now, at Mom's place, waiting for the phone to ring, I sat on my bed holding my book and looked over at the clock once more. It was three, and the phone was still silent. *He doesn't care.* Now I was angry. *I'm here waiting and waiting for the phone to ring. I can't even call him, because he said it was a work day for him and it would be easier for him to call me. So I'm sitting here and I can't do anything. He is just doing whatever he is doing but he isn't calling me. We made an arrangement and he doesn't care! I loved him. How could I be such a fool?*

I went to the kitchen, where my Mom was preparing dinner. I couldn't recall the last time I went to her when

I was feeling in need. With my head down, I said, "Mom, I feel so…." I searched for the feeling as if it were somewhere on the floor. I had been feeling angry, but there was something else there, and I didn't recognise it until it came out of my mouth, "…sad." That was it. I was feeling sad, deeply sad. The anger was covering up the sadness.

My mother took my face in her hands like only a mother can and looked into my eyes. "Oh honey, it hurts doesn't it?" she said gently. She didn't even know what I was sad about. She just felt my sadness and acknowledged it. That was all I needed. A depth of grief that I didn't even know was there spilled out of me along with the tears.

I was sad about my marriage. I was sad about losing my friends. I was sad about leaving the farm. I was sad about Daniel. I was sad that I hadn't let my Mom hold me like this before. I was sad about my Dad.

My mother held me while I sobbed, and I let her. I didn't pull away. There was no more resistance inside me. Only love.

It was four o'clock when Daniel finally called. He sincerely apologised and said he had been busy. It was nice to hear his voice. He reminded me of my father.

Mom said she and Dad were soulmates, but that they just needed to separate when they did. It happened not long after Dad forgot to pick me up from swimming. His bad days got worse, and years later, he did the unthinkable. He took his life. It rocked my world. By then I had learned not to rely on him for anything, but somewhere deep in my heart he had still been my hero, and he was gone.

"Take care and travel safely back to New Zealand," Daniel said at the end of our call.

I sniffed and wiped my tears. "Yes I will. You take care too. Good-bye."

Chapter 30

Sitting on the plane, I rested my fingers on the ledge of the window. *That was the longest and the shortest visit with my mother I have ever had.* I usually visited every two years for a couple of weeks, and often by the end I was itching to leave. This time we experienced so much together, and for the first time, I was truly sad to leave. I could have stayed longer.

Looking out at the blue sky and clouds, I was lost in my daydreams, reliving all my adventures, the miracles, the new friends I made. I wondered how it would feel to be back in New Zealand after all this. *Will I see things from a different perspective? What kind of life will I create around me now?*

I was grateful that I had arranged to stay at a retreat centre for my first few days back. It would give me a chance to integrate the things I had learned on my travels before I had to deal with the practical business of starting a new life for myself.

Pushing the luggage trolley, I looked at the familiar blue line painted on the walkway guiding me from the Auckland international terminal to the domestic terminal. I had walked this path many times before.

I lifted my face to the sky, allowing the cool New Zealand air to soothe my skin. It felt so good after all the summer heat I'd had.

So this is home. I imagined myself wriggling into my favourite old jacket. I took in a deep breath and rolled my shoulders up and down. *What does it feel like to be back?* My awareness moved to the bushes alongside the walkway. I had expected to greet them like an old friend, but when I looked at them, something wasn't right.

I tipped my head to the side and stared. I had seen these bushes many times before, and they had always felt familiar to me. *Why aren't they familiar now?* I started to feel uneasy.

I reached out to touch the leaves. I thought maybe if I connected with them in a more tactile way that might make a difference. I wanted to feel some comfort, to feel at home. But the plant stayed silent and separate from me. I felt no connection.

I stepped back and let go. Something was wrong. *I feel as if I am in a foreign country.* Now I was feeling a bit scared. My eyes searched all the plants along the walkway, thinking maybe it was just this one bush, but they all looked foreign.

Then I had a horrible thought.

"Is this not my home anymore?" I whispered to the bushes. No answer.

It was like being in a nightmare in which I had arrived at what I thought was my house only to find out that it wasn't my house and in fact I didn't have a house anymore.

I felt completely alone.

The next day just before dawn I sat outside wrapped in my shawl surrounded by the trees and bushes at the retreat centre. A cool breeze brushed my face. I closed my eyes. The first bird chirped. I sat very still, not wanting to ask the question that was waiting to be asked.

The light had just begun to break. The wind whistled through the tall trees. Looking up, I watched their branches sway gracefully in surrender to the force. I released the question I had held back in my mind, already knowing the answer. I closed my eyes with a shudder and asked, "I'm moving back to Canada, aren't I?"

Feeling like I had arrived in a foreign country shook me deeply. As I reflected on it, I felt that maybe it was true. Maybe New Zealand was no longer the place for me to call home.

The breath of the wind rose. "Yes," the wind whispered through the trees.

"Okay." I bowed my head in surrender. I pulled my shawl around me closer and silenced a hair-ripping scream expressing my horror at the idea of uprooting and re-establishing myself after twenty-three years in New Zealand.

Three weeks earlier, when exploring Boynton Canyon in Sedona, I was sitting on a ledge of the big red rock with my legs dangling. The mid-day summer sun warmed the top of my head as I looked out over the vast, dry red desert. I was reflecting on the message I had received from Stonehenge telling me it was time to fly. I wondered what it meant and decided to go to an expert for help.

Closing my eyes, I relaxed into a meditative state. I

called in Eagle and in my mind I saw a very large eagle land on the ledge just above me. As if in a dream, I began to interact with it.

> *"Eagle, will you teach me how to fly?"*
>
> *Eagle glanced at me and nodded. Then it looked straight ahead for a moment, as if contemplating where to start. It communicated with me telepathically in thought forms.*
>
> *"First, never take off unless you know where you are going."* What a good point.
>
> *"Once you are in the air, stay alert as you look for opportunities, and be flexible enough to change course if an opportunity arises."*
>
> *A vision appeared before me of a bird flying towards a branch. It spotted an insect and immediately darted towards the insect, then flew on, landing on a different branch than the one it had originally aimed for.*
>
> *I imagined how ridiculous it would be if birds always had to end up at the destinations they aimed for. I envisaged them bumping into each other, unable to alter their course, and making redundant flights with the only purpose of landing on the original target.*

I was stunned by the simplicity and depth of this lesson. And I was challenged by how to interpret it, because my human logic told me that it was fickle to change my course every time a better opportunity arose.

Spreading its wings, Eagle lifted up to fly, leaving me with one last message.

Now, huddled in my shawl at the retreat centre in New Zealand, reflecting on the message I had just received to move back to Canada, I repeated his words:

"Hold the vision. Let go of the plan."

Chapter 31

Standing in the doorway of my half-empty storage unit, I watched the two young men who won the online auction carry away my beloved handmade green couches.

There was a story behind each item in that small space, and I had expected to feel sad watching them being taken away, but I didn't. *Maybe I'm too numb to feel anything.* I smiled. I knew that wasn't true. I didn't feel any regret or even uncertainty watching my belongings leave with their new owners. I felt calm and excited. Just like when I sold my set of good quality pots and pans to my friends who now rented me a room. I would stay with them as a flatmate until I left for Canada, and I was happy my pots were going to a good home.

Letting go of material things was easy, but my heart ached thinking about saying goodbye to New Zealand, to my friends and the abundant life I had lived here. With my departure date planned for February I had just over two months to say all of my goodbyes.

Christmas was quickly approaching, and for the past several years I had attended a festival over the holiday period. Miriam and I usually either went together or met up at the gathering. This time we would meet there. The festival attracted anywhere from thirty to sixty people, often the same core group, and they had become like family. This would be my last time with them.

As I made the five-hour drive to the event, a throbbing ache grew in my chest, and I tried not to think about the goodbyes coming soon. The sun was just setting when I arrived, and as I drove up the familiar driveway I smiled recalling the many moments spent laughing, singing, dancing, crying, and sharing in that place. It felt so good to be there.

The manager of the retreat centre came out to welcome me and show me to the small, round caravan where I would be staying for the next ten days. The centre had many kinds of accommodation including cottages, shared rooms, tents and caravans. Over the years I had tried them all, except this one.

"It's gorgeous!" I exclaimed.

It was painted a rich green, and with a slight shift in perspective it could have passed for a green toadstool, the humble dwelling of an elf.

The next morning I lay in bed surveying my toadstool caravan in the light of day. The bed wasn't a single and wasn't a double, but somewhere in-between; a divan just big enough for my suitcase and to display all of my tops for easy selection; a little table by the bed for my crystal and notebook; and some shelves for miscellaneous items. Everything had a place. I felt like a little bird in its nest, safe and held.

Thinking about all the people who would be arriving soon, my hand went to my belly and it felt noticeably peaceful. I thought of Miriam who would arrive tomorrow—I hadn't seen her since before my trip. I even thought about the people who would expect Martin to be there with me, and still my belly was calm. I didn't expect Martin to be there—events like these were usually more my thing—and to my knowledge he hadn't contacted any of these people, apart from Miriam.

I had expected to feel some anxious abdominal pain as I usually did but it wasn't there. In the past at this festival, it sometimes took me a couple of days to settle down before I felt still inside again. This time I felt present and relaxed right from the beginning.

Maybe because I was leaving, I didn't care so much what people thought. Or maybe I felt much more whole and confident in myself after all my adventures. In any case, it was wonderful to feel peaceful, alive and present.

I got dressed and went to the big hall. When I stepped inside, everything was quiet, except for a few murmurs coming from the kitchen. A door creaked open and I looked down the corridor. A tall man with light brown hair and blue eyes smiled at me. I had noticed him the evening before when I arrived.

"Good morning!" I said, expressing the joy and peace I felt inside but also trying to cover up a little bit of nervousness I felt in seeing him. *Why am I feeling nervous? Am I wondering if he finds me attractive?* I took in a deep breath, and as I exhaled all anxiousness left me. I smiled, feeling grounded again.

We hugged. Hugging was the handshake used at this gathering. Everyone was so friendly and warm with each other it seemed the natural thing to do. Some hugs were 'A-frame': the kind where your feet are kept a good distance apart from the other person's and only the top halves of your bodies lean in. Other hugs were more warm and embracing, with more parts of the body connected. This hug definitely rated in the latter category.

My body completely relaxed in his arms, and a warm current of energy flowed briefly between us. I felt it in the centre of my chest. *Oh my goodness, I like this guy.* I didn't really want to like anybody, but the deliciousness of attraction was irresistible.

"Mmmmm," he said as we released ourselves from the hug. "I'm coming in for another one." With a big smile on his face, Richard stepped forward for another delicious hug.

"That's a lovely good morning hug," I said, trying to regain my composure. A part of me wanted to collapse and swoon in his arms while another part, a more responsible part, was telling me to steer clear of him, because I was in no position to be falling for someone.

Over the next couple of days, the community grew as people came from all around the country and from overseas: South America, Germany, Holland, the United States and Canada. There were lots of hugs and plenty of excited chatter as I met new people and greeted old friends. Throughout it all, a lovely, warm tingling lingered in my body, and I couldn't get Richard out of my mind.

"Knock. Knock." The little door of my caravan was softly tapped. "What are you wearing?" a women's voice called out.

"Your timing is perfect," I said, opening the door. Miriam's tall frame stepped in. Even though we had been through so much over our sixteen years of friendship—including now our most recent conversation of betrayal and forgiveness—I had often felt intimidated by her. Was it her strong physical presence? Or was it that she was so eloquent with words? But this time there was no judgmental chatter in my mind or feelings of inadequacy. I felt fantastically okay in myself, and genuinely happy to see her.

My fingers were twisting and straining as I attempted to do up the laces at the back of my red velvet dress. After she had done my ties, Miriam held two scarves up to her neck. "Which one goes better with my dress?" she asked. I chose the blue one for her, and with that settled we made our way towards the hall for the big Christmas dinner.

My stomach fluttered when we entered the dining room. I looked around for Richard, wondering if he would like my dress. I saw a tall figure in my peripheral vision. I turned. He was looking right at me. I blushed. He smiled. *He is so good looking.*

Miriam and I found seats that overlooked the whole dining room. From time to time I glanced up from my conversations to peek at Richard. Every time he was looking at me, and every time I blushed. I felt as if my cheeks were beacons blaring my attraction for him, and I wriggled, feeling deliciously uncomfortable.

I had left a bottle of sparkling grape juice in the fridge at the back of the kitchen, and I went outside to get it. As I stepped out of the walk-in refrigerator, the ties of my dress caught on the door handle and came undone. Just at that moment, Richard came along the path at the back of the kitchen.

I rolled my eyes at the timing of the universe. It was like a staged moment.

"Richard, would you please do up the ties on my dress?" I said, feeling ridiculous but also a bit giddy.

He laughed. "With pleasure," he said. I turned my back to him and showed him the laces. His body was close behind mine. As he fumbled with the ties, his fingers brushed the skin on my back. Tingles sparked up and down my spine with every touch. Desire for him swept through me.

"I'm not sure if I'm doing this right," he said. He was genuinely having trouble. Then with some exasperation he exhaled and said, "Oh why am I trying to do these up when I'd rather be undoing them!" He let the ties go and wrapped his arms around my waist from behind. I started to giggle and just then the back door swung open and someone came out. We both quickly stepped apart, laughing like two teenagers caught out. My face all flushed, I dashed inside to find some real help with my dress.

Every time Richard and I passed one another that night, I felt an electrical current flow through me. It was feverish and tantalising.

The next day, I was sitting outside enjoying the sun and chatting with a woman I had just met. She looked up just as Richard came to join us on the picnic bench, and in her direct and playful way she said, "There's some kind of attraction going on between you two, isn't there?"

Why would she say that in front of him? I felt embarrassed.

Is it that obvious to other people? I started to feel panicky as the blood rushed to my cheeks again. *Oh no! Relax. Relax.* The last thing I wanted was to come across like a needy woman who was head-over-heels. All my powerful adventures and deep insights were not helping me now.

Richard smiled, "Yes.".

I relaxed a little, and my red cheeks bobbed up and down in agreement as I looked at him. I wondered what it meant now that it was out in the open. Suddenly my mind was filled with conflict. *Will he ask me out? But I don't want to be asked out. Yes I do. But I'm leaving. I don't need a relationship. But it feels so good. I hope something happens.*

I remembered the hypnotherapy session with Isobelle and my Higher Self's clear message. "She doesn't need and she doesn't desire to be in a relationship." It was still true that I didn't need to be in a relationship. I felt so strong and good inside myself. I didn't need anyone to supplement me.

The following day while making my way to my caravan, I saw Richard wave and come toward me. "Would you like to go for a swim?" He knew a private swimming place on the lake.

My heart leapt, but trying to keep my voice even and casual, I said, "Sure."

"Great. I'll come and find you at two o'clock," He sauntered away.

I stood there staring after him, probably with my mouth hanging open. His confidence was breath-taking. *I think I've just been asked out on a date.* Feeling lightheaded, I floated back to my caravan.

As we hiked through the bush to the swimming hole, Richard took my hand, and a warm tingling went through me again. I didn't feel in control at all, but I was loving the surprise of each moment, and it all felt so natural.

A big flat rock jutted out over the large crater-lake, and we sat down on a smooth spot. The warmth of the sun emanating from the rock was wonderfully soothing. Richard's hand reached out to caress my face. His head leaned in. His lips found mine. Contact. The surge of energy began to flow through me again, and I knew it was flowing through him, too.

Do I want to fall in love? Is this the time for that? The faint voice in my mind was quickly drowned by my heart. My eyes met his, and I felt my heart open wide. I could have sat there all day, drunk with joy, just looking into his eyes.

"I'm moving to Canada, you realise."

"I know."

"You might want to get to know some other lovely woman who isn't going away."

"I quite like spending time with you."

Over the next few days, our romance flourished, but I couldn't stop thinking about the future. I tried to tell myself that it was just a fling, but it didn't feel like a fling at all. When I thought about the possibility that I might never see him again if I moved back to Canada, I felt a painful wrench in my heart.

You are not leaving right now, Leanne. I practiced reminding myself to stay in the present moment so that

I could enjoy the time we had, and enjoy ourselves we did.

Chapter 32

When I stepped out of the creek, fresh from a swim in the cold water, Richard's eyes twinkled as he said, "I didn't think a city girl would like it here that much."

Richard lived on a five-acre lifestyle block with chickens, horses and a lively creek running through the backyard. It was heaven. *When I settle back in Canada, I want to live in a place just like this.* My heart gripped in my chest as my thoughts flickered again to leaving New Zealand. Then I looked into Richard's smiling face and blue eyes and all the sadness disappeared.

It was a hot summer day, and I had just over a month left in the country. Given how little time we had, we were spending as much of it as possible together. Our plan for the evening was to go to the local pizza place. It was our first proper date, and I was a bit disappointed that he hadn't chosen something more special, but I didn't say anything.

"We'll have to take the ladder with us," he said. "The waders won't work with your skirt." My eyes opened wide. *Waders? What is he talking about?*

"What do you mean?" I asked.

"Well, we have to cross a river to get there, and the water will be up to our thighs. We could walk across in waders, but not with your skirt. There's a bridge that's for council use only, but if we take my ladder, we can climb over the security gate and cross the bridge."

I was even less impressed than I had been to start with.

Half an hour later, we stood in front of a ten-foot-high barbed wire gate. *I'm going to climb over this so I can have some pizza?* I gathered up my skirt and cautiously, ungracefully made my way up the ladder, all the while muttering to myself that I should have worn jeans.

Richard helped me down on the other side, and when he took my hand, I forgot my annoyance about the unexpected mountaineering. I was with him, and I was blissfully happy.

As we walked along a dirt road, it looked like we were going absolutely nowhere except deeper into the countryside. Then at the end of a long, thin driveway that veered off the dirt road stood a stunningly beautiful, hand-crafted wooden chalet with fairy-lights around all the windows and the roof frame. It looked like a real gingerbread house. The property was sustainably powered by solar panels and hydroelectricity from the creek that ran alongside it. This enchanted hobbit-house was the local organic pizza joint.

Who would have guessed a place like this existed out here?

It was only open on Friday evenings, when people from all over the neighbourhood, and some from around New Zealand, came for traditional thin-crust pizza made from flour ground right there in an old-fashioned stone mill. We were lucky to get a seat, and when I took my first bite of blue cheese, walnut and pear pizza, I understood why.

What a surprise it had all been. I looked down at my boots scuffed with mud from our journey and felt glad that my judgments hadn't held me back.

Each moment with Richard was exhilarating. We went on road trips, camped, swam, canoed, hiked, danced, went to community gatherings. We laughed till we cried and we cried till we laughed. The days passed, and the more I fell in love, the more I agonised about leaving.

One morning, I sat cross-legged on the bed in the room I was renting from my friends, and spoke the lines of a poem that resonated with me. I wanted to hear the words out loud and see how it felt to speak them, like a mantra. "I release all hopes." I wanted to let go of hoping for things to be different. I had expected some resistance to that, but there wasn't any. In fact I felt relief when I said it.

"I release all desires." I quite liked my desires, but that one felt easy too. Feeling encouraged, I eagerly continued.

"I release all dreams." Thud. A door slammed shut inside of me. I didn't want to release my dreams. I wanted my dreams. I *needed* them. Then I remembered the five eagles playing in the air in the Grand Canyon. Their lesson to me was to practice *conscious intention, focused effort and let go.*

I tried again. "I release all dreams." I felt something shift inside. I moved on to the last part of the poem.

"I release all expectations."

As I said the whole mantra again altogether, I could feel my worry and concern fall away. I felt more present and more accepting of how things were. Everything was as it should be. My heart calmed down, I breathed easily and I felt peaceful.

By the time February arrived, I had decided to extend my departure date, reasoning that it would be better to leave at the end of March, after the North American winter. After another few weeks of fun and bliss with Richard, I decided that April would be a much better time to go, and my friends were still happy for me to be their flatmate.

I didn't want to leave the love I had found, but then I couldn't stay in New Zealand either. I had spent so much time practicing listening to my intuition. *How could I possibly go against the message I had received? What could I do?*

I decided to head back into nature to find some answers.

I went into a field behind the house where I was staying and looked for the same kind of bush that had looked strange to me when I arrived at Auckland Airport. I found one easily and went to sit by it. After taking a few moments to relax and to get into a meditative space, I asked. "Why were you so foreign to me?"

"You were not recognised. You were not the same person you were when you left," it said.

I shook my head. It wasn't the plant that was foreign. It was me.

Then I asked the big question, the one I really needed

to have answered. "Where should I live? In New Zealand or in Canada?"

The answer that came was perfect, but very unhelpful. The bush said, "You will create community and love wherever you are. It doesn't matter where you choose to live."

Am I still welcome here?

"Yes."

Two paths had just opened up before me, but I didn't want to choose. I wanted a clear sign.

Sighing, I lay back on the grass and said to the blue sky, "I release all hopes, desires, dreams and expectations." I relaxed a little more. The sun warmed and soothed my skin.

I remembered saying goodbye to my mother at the airport in Toronto, eight months earlier. We were both crying, thinking that once I went through the doors to airport security, we wouldn't see each other for at least another two years.

Then I got the call to return to Canada. Mom was so happy. She would be heartbroken if I changed my mind, and I would feel really sad.

On the other hand, I so wanted to stay in New Zealand and continue to experience this joyful union with Richard. I closed my eyes and imagined myself saying goodbye to him, and a pain jabbed at my heart. I felt overcome with regret, wondering if I would ever find such a love again.

No matter what I chose there would be great sadness

and disappointment. "I don't know what to do," I said out loud to the clouds.

Deep in my heart, though, I did.

Chapter 33

The grass was soft under my feet as my body swayed to the seductive beat of South American tunes pulsing from the stereo speakers. Richard and I were dancing on his lawn. He dipped me back into a dancers' embrace, and my heart felt like it would explode with joy.

Later, when we were sitting across from each other at the kitchen table, I took his hands and looked deeply into his eyes. "I'm not going to move to Canada," I said. "I'm going to stay in New Zealand."

I hadn't made my decision lightly. I had taken the time to be at peace with my choice. I loved New Zealand, and I loved this man. What better place to be than with all of that love?

Richard quickly pulled his hands away and fear flashed through his eyes. "You can't stay because of me," he said. "If things don't work out between us, it will be my fault that you stayed."

I had expected him to be happy and excited like me, but I understood his fear.

"Oh my love," I said. "I can move back to Canada anytime I want. If things don't work out and we separate, we'll have had this wonderful time together, for however long it lasts. You are not responsible for my life."

His face softened, and he stood up opening his

arms to me and wrapping them around me, our bodies melted together.

Lying in bed the next morning, snuggled into sheets still warm from our body heat, I felt perfectly content. Then I looked out of the window. The sun was already high in the sky. *Late morning again.* I breathed a sigh of disappointment.

Richard had gone to make us both a hot lemon drink and was bringing them back to bed. *I really should get up and do my morning practices.* But I didn't move. I wanted to be there when Richard returned.

It had been months since I had done my morning practices with any regularity. Sometimes I forgot them completely. I frowned, recalling the previous week, when I wasn't at Richard's. I woke up at four in the morning every day to meditate and pray before sunrise, and then take a brisk walk. I loved those rituals for greeting the day. They helped me to feel grounded and clear inside. I was missing them.

Closing my eyes, I rolled over and waited for Richard to come back.

The next morning as we lay in bed, the song of chirping birds called me, and I opened my eyes. I glanced over at Richard's face. His eyes were still closed. I felt the desire to get up and do my practices, but I didn't move.

A niggle of resentment stirred inside me. *It's much easier not being in a relationship. I can do what I want and not worry if I am pleasing someone or not. No one can question my actions or my decisions. There are no hurt feelings or misunderstandings. Being on my own is more freeing!*

I looked over at him sleeping next to me. I hadn't even told him about my frustrations, and I had never asked him if he expected me to stay in bed with him all morning. He had no idea what was going on in my head, and I was busy making assumptions about what was going on in his.

The insight continued to unravel. *This is how I do it! This is how I compromise myself.* I began to see so clearly how I had repeated the pattern in failed relationship after failed relationship. I compromised myself based on some assumption about what was expected of me, and over time I became more and more resentful, but I said nothing until the bitterness had closed my heart. When I finally ended those relationships, relieved that I no longer had to live with so much compromise, it never occurred to me that my own assumptions had been the cause.

As I pondered this deep revelation, I felt something release inside. It wasn't about finding the right guy who was going to do all the right things. It was about me claiming my space to be myself without compromising what was important to me. *Is there such a thing as relationship without compromise?*

Now, I couldn't imagine it working any other way.

I remembered the Rumi poem about facing the fire, and I rolled over to look at Richard. He opened his eyes and smiled at me lovingly. My heart flipped, and in the next second I gasped with fear. I was afraid of losing him.

My fingers clenched my palms and tears filled my

eyes as I shared my thoughts, my fears and my insights. As I continued to speak, the fear shifted to relief and then to a sense of deep inner strength, and in that strength I no longer feared how he would respond.

When I had finished speaking, Richard pulled the bed covers back and pushed me out of bed. "Go do your practices," he said, laughing. "The more you do what you want, the more you are going to love me."

He was right.

Chapter 34

My trowel slid easily into the ground as I dug a hole for the lavender plant. *I love the smell of the earth.* I moved the dirt aside with my hands and eased the little bundle into its new home. I was settling into my new home living at Richard's.

My fingers worked the displaced earth around the plant and patted the soil very gently to secure it in place. I picked up the watering can, and as I watered all the flowers I had just planted, I imagined their roots happy and alive, establishing themselves, just like me.

Opening the kitchen door I looked at the clock. Four-thirty. I smiled. *Where has the time gone?* I put down the watering can, peeled off my sticky clothes and headed for the creek for a swim. When the cool, refreshing water met my skin, I was in heaven.

I loved living at Richard's house, tending and harvesting and cooking food from the gardens, swimming in the creek, lying on the lawn under the stars at night. It was paradise, but even paradise had its downsides.

The house was so far out in the country that Internet access was not possible, and even cell phone coverage was intermittent. Whenever I received a call, I had to jump into any pair of shoes I could find, usually Richard's, and run down the road, shoes flapping at my heels, hoping to find better coverage.

I depended on regular Internet access for my work, so every day I had to drive four kilometres up the road—where there was enough cell phone coverage—pull over onto the corner of a farmer's paddock, and set up my mobile office in the backseat of my car. This was not ideal for many reasons, but the biggest was that I could only work as long as my bladder could hold out.

Two days a week, I embarked on the two-hour-long drive to the city to work with clients face-to-face. Sometimes I returned on the same day, and sometimes I stayed overnight with friends. When I wasn't commuting up the road or into town, I was packing and unpacking my car and constantly looking for places where I could stay overnight. It took an enormous amount of effort to make it all work.

Occasionally, Richard and I talked about buying property together closer to the city, but we always reached a stalemate. He loved his paradise, and I didn't blame him. He also admitted that he loved living on his own and had done so for most of his life. "Although I'm quite happy with you staying here right now," he quickly said.

One morning, I was sitting alone on the two-seater cane couch on the side porch. The new branches and new green leaves were sprouting on the trees, and the lawn was strewn with petals. Spring was bursting with energy after a cold winter. As I picked up my mug of tea, my fingers strained under the weight of the full cup. I didn't have much energy.

Settling back into the cushions again I noticed a niggle in my heart. It had been there for a while but I hadn't wanted to look. A big, old wisteria had gorgeously wound its way up one of the pillars of the porch. Its many new shoots were reaching out and bobbing their heads in the breeze as if to encourage me to look.

I sighed. I felt unhappy.

But how can that be? I am in a wonderful relationship, living the life of my dreams and still managing to get all of my work done. How can I be unhappy?

It hadn't yet occurred to me that it was taking every ounce of energy and attention I had just to hold all the parts of my life together. There was nothing left. My tank was empty. I had no capacity for play, for fun, for creating, for listening, for talking with the trees.

This was not how I wanted to live.

My eyes explored the wisteria vine. The strong trunk was thicker than my arms and had been growing for fifteen years. The bundles of flowers bloomed abundantly along the whole plant. I knew the question I wanted to ask.

"Why am I unhappy?" I asked the plant in my mind. My attention was immediately drawn to two birds on the front lawn. They were doing a courtship dance, and soon they would be making a nest that would hold and take care of their eggs. For a moment I felt sad.

Then I had another thought which took me by surprise. *I am not holding and taking care of myself.* I had been nurturing my relationship and my career at the expense of my own needs. *I have forgotten about me — again!*

The insights continued to unfold as I watched the agile new shoots of the wisteria happily waving more energetically in the wind. *I need to make a nest for me. I need to find a home that works for me. If Richard doesn't want to be a part of that, I need to do it on my own.*

I picked up a cushion, held it tightly to my chest and whispered, "What does this mean?" *Do we have to separate? We can't separate! We love each other!* My breath had quickened along with my heart.

For an instant I imagined myself continuing the way I had been, with all the travel and logistical problems. My whole body felt like a dead weight, but underneath the heaviness was a river of resentment flowing though my veins.

I have to move.

As soon as I had this thought, I felt relieved and even excited, but then I thought of Richard. *How is he going to take this?*

I was nervous but I decided to speak to him that afternoon rather than follow an old pattern of keeping my feelings to myself. Richard was in the kitchen finishing up the dishes from lunch. "I've been thinking about something and I want to talk it over with you," I said pulling out a chair at the table and sitting down. I could feel my heart beating.

Richard rinsed out the dish rag, hung it on the tap and came to join me.

I held my own hands as I looked into his eyes. *Will he think I don't want to be with him? Will he decide this is all too hard and end the relationship now?* I could feel the tears pushing behind my eyes. *It doesn't have to mean breaking up.* I took a deep breath.

"Richard, I've been really struggling and haven't been willing to admit it because I love you and I love being here so much. I'm also afraid of sharing this with you because of what it might mean for us." I closed my eyes. *Don't cry. Don't cry. Too late. I began to cry and in-between my tears I managed to say,* "I have to get my own place closer to the city and I don't want to break up."

I shared with him how hard it had been, that I was exhausted and I just couldn't keep doing it.

Richard put his head down and nodded. His eyes filled with tears as he said, "I'm sorry it has been so difficult. Sometimes I felt so helpless knowing I couldn't fix things for you." Then he shook his head. "I don't know if it can work with us not living close by."

No! Don't give up! My mind was screaming as I said, "This doesn't mean that we can't still be together. I love you. I love us."

I reminded myself of the flying eagles' message again. *Hold conscious intention, focused effort and then let go. Richard will make his own choice.* I took a deep breath, and let it go.

"Well, I guess other people live apart and are still a couple," he said. "I will be sad because I have loved having you here living with me, but I understand. I don't know how it will work but I'm sure we'll figure it out." He looked into my eyes and reached for my hands.

I squeezed his hands as my heart burst open with love for us. I knew we were going to be okay.

In the weeks that followed, all my attention was on finding a new nest for myself. In no time, I found a lovely house in a country town not too far from Wellington. It felt a little strange getting my own place again. It wasn't my dream to live by myself. I still wanted to live with my partner and to share land with others. But for now I knew that this was my next step, and it felt right.

I wondered what would have happened if I had gone back to Canada. *I'd probably be in a similar situation needing to find a home.* I shuddered thinking about the challenges involved in a move like that: finding a place to live, setting up my business all over again, and creating new networks and friends. *I'm so glad I didn't go. I don't want to leave New Zealand. I don't want to leave Richard.*

But on the other hand, maybe Canada would have offered more opportunities. What if doing my work and getting more business was easier there? And what if I experienced that feeling of deep belonging that can only be experienced when one returns to the place of one's birth—like when a square peg finds its square hole.

I shook my head. *Well, I will never know.*

It took Richard and me a whole day and a big trailer to pick up a bed, a table, a filing cabinet and a refrigerator, all from different locations, and move everything over the mountains to my new home.

At the end of the day, standing on the threshold of the front door of my new house, I put the key in the lock and paused. This moment heralded a new phase in our relationship. *Are we going backwards or forwards?* I remembered the message from Bell Rock, the stone I had climbed in Sedona, "Sometimes you have to go back to go forward."

It all felt right. I opened the door.

Too tired to set up the bed, we dropped the mattress on the bedroom floor, threw some sheets on it and fell asleep.

The next morning I opened my eyes and looked over at Richard. He was still sleeping.

Breathing in deeply, all I felt was love and my wide open heart.

I propped up my head with my hand and Richard opened his eyes and smiled. I was so grateful for his help and his love. We lay there looking at each other, saying nothing with our words and everything with our eyes like we had done so many times before.

In the silence, my mind began to chatter. *Will we make it? Will we live happily ever after?* My mind wanted everything nailed down and figured out, but my spirit didn't need that.

I looked deeply into his beautiful blue eyes again and breathed into the centre of my chest. I felt no attachment to being in a relationship with him at all, and yet I loved him. Strangely, there was no yearning, pulling or fear. This was new for me. I hadn't felt like this before. I checked inside again just to make sure, but there was no fear or desire to hold on to anything. Instead, there was only a feeling of peace.

I felt vulnerable and yet very strong at the same time, like I could handle anything, not from being stoic but from being so open, resilient and resisting nothing.

I knew everything was going to be okay, no matter how things unfolded, whether we were together or apart.

I was free.

The bushes rustled outside, calling my attention, as if whispering, "That's right."

During breakfast we made plans to catch up on the weekend. Then Richard left for the two hour drive back to his place. I made myself a cup of tea and went outside to sit in the garden. The wind whistled through the tall trees. Looking up, I watched their branches swaying gracefully in surrender to the force. A billowing gust rose as if it was taking in a deep breath to speak.

I closed my eyes and felt its breath. Then the wind whispered in my ear.

I knew what it was going to say before I heard it.

I nodded. "Yes," I said softly bowing my head in total surrender.

I opened my eyes. Everything was quiet. I pulled my shawl around me closer, and this time there was no hair-ripping scream to silence. There weren't even any thoughts in my head like: *But you just bought this place. How can you think of leaving?* I wasn't afraid. No matter what happened, this *was* the journey, and everything was going to be okay.

Closing my eyes again I brought Eagle to mind and imagined him speaking to me, saying, "Hold your vision. Let go of your plans, and—fly."

So that was what I did.

Keeping in touch

Leanne offers courses, retreats and one-on-one coaching or healing sessions. You can keep in touch and find out about events she is offering simply by going to: www.leannebabcock.ca and sign up for the newsletter.

To find out where she's at with her travels visit:

www. leannebabcock.ca

You can also follow Leanne on:

www.facebook.com/openmebook

www.instagram.com/leannebabcock

www.twitter.com/Leannebabcock

If you'd like to know more about the book, *Open Me*, and hear what others are saying, then check out:

www.facebook.com/openmebook

Did you enjoy your read?

If you'd like to write a review we'd love to hear from you. Please go to:

www.Amazon.ca

Or the website from where you purchased the book.